HAUNTED
WEARSIDE

St Peter's Church, Monkwearmouth, said to be haunted by ghostly monks. (Courtesy of Newcastle Libraries and Information Service)

HAUNTED
WEARSIDE

Darren W. Ritson

The
History
Press

This book is dedicated to my good friend

Michael J. Hallowell

First published 2013

The History Press
The Mill, Brimscombe Port
Stroud, Gloucestershire, GL5 2QG
www.thehistorypress.co.uk

© Darren W. Ritson, 2013

The right of Darren W. Ritson to be identified as the Author
of this work has been asserted in accordance with the
Copyright, Designs and Patents Act 1988.

British Library Cataloguing in Publication Data.
A catalogue record for this book is available from the British Library.

ISBN 978 0 7524 6088 8
Typesetting and origination by The History Press
Printed in Great Britain

CONTENTS

ACKNOWLEDGEMENTS

T0 Mike Hallowell for his usual help and support. To England's Lost Country Houses for allowing the image of Herrington Hall to be published in this book; visit their website at www.lostheritage.org.uk, thanks Matthew. To the Newcastle Libraries and Information Service for the use of other certain images produced herein, to Julie Olley for her amazing illustrations that she has provided for inclusion, and to everyone else that has played their small part in helping me compile this book, you know who you are ...

ALSO BY THE AUTHOR

The South Shields Poltergeist, One Family's Fight against an Invisible Intruder (With
    Michael J. Hallowell, Sutton Publishing, 2008, 2009)
Haunted Newcastle (2009)
Haunted Durham (2010)
Haunted Berwick (2010)
Ghosts at Christmas (2010)
Haunted Northumberland (2011)
The Haunting of Willington Mill (With Michael J. Hallowell, 2011)
Haunted Tyneside (2011)
Haunted Carlisle (2012)

INTRODUCTION

FOR many years I had yearned to pen a volume on the ghosts and spectres of Wearside, and in 2012 I was given the chance to do so. After writing other paranormal related books on my native north east of England, such as *Haunted Tyneside, Haunted Northumberland, Haunted Newcastle, Haunted Durham, Haunted Berwick*, and even *Haunted Carlisle*, I decided that it was time to venture across to Wearside to investigate and collate true-life accounts of ghosts, poltergeists and things that go bump in the night, thus placing them all under one metaphorical roof. Wearside seems to be a magnet for ghosts and spirits with many of its old and historical buildings and lands seemingly occupied by denizens of the Otherworld; shades from a time gone by determined to make their unearthly presence known to an ever-growing modern day society. Of course, one of the most famous tales of the supernatural associated with Wearside is that of the Lambton Worm.

A stone carving depicting the killing of the Lambton Worm by John Lambton after his return from the crusades.

For those unaware of this narrative I shall briefly outline it here; the tale centres around John Lambton who, one day, decided to miss Sunday Mass and go fishing instead, but was approached by a mysterious old man who warned him that no good can come of missing church. John went fishing nonetheless and caught nothing until the time of the church service finishing, where-upon he netted a strange-looking eel-like creature. On his way home, he decided to throw this creature down a local well and forgot all about it. When John grew up, he left England and went to join the crusades in the Holy Lands. In the meanwhile, growing down the well was the serpent-like creature that he had caught in the River Wear all those years ago.

By all accounts, this creature was getting bigger and stronger each day that went by, as it ventured out of the well at night and ate local livestock. Eventually, the creature that became known as the Lambton Worm was too big to live in the well and relocated down by the river, where he sat upon a huge rock. Sometimes he would wrap himself round a nearby hill which give the hillside a strange, bevelled edge; edges that can still be seen today if you believe the myth. The hill was said by some to be Penshaw Hill, but others are not so sure − they think the hill is an embankment in nearby Fatfield, known locally as 'Worm Hill'.

The creature caused mischief and mayhem for many years, and ter-rorised the good folk of Wearside. Upon his return from the crusades, John Lambton learned all about the creature. He decided to take on the mighty beast, but not before seeking

Penshaw Hill and Monument. Some folk suggest this was where the Lambton Worm rested as it wrapped itself round the hill.

Right *A street sign bearing the name 'Worm Hill Terrace' that runs alongside the hill in Fatfield.*

Below *Worm Hill in Fatfield. Some have suggested that the beast rested and slept on this hillock.*

advice from a local wise woman. The first thing she told him was that the Lambton Worm was *his* doing, and this made him more determined to take the beast down. She then told him to fight the monster with a specially made suit of armour that bore spikes, and to fight the beast down by the river. Finally, she said that after he had killed the beast, it was essential that he then slayed the first living thing he laid his eyes on, otherwise the Lambton family would be cursed for many generations to come with 'none of them dying in their beds'.

Upon returning to the Lambton Estate, he hatched a plan to have one of the Lambton hounds released, so that he could kill the dog after slaying the creature and be free from any curse. All the servant had to do was listen out for the hunting horn and release the hound. Off John went, down to the river, suited and booted, ready to kill the beast. He found the monster curled around the huge rock and fronted up to it. Soon the battle was in full swing and every time the beast tried to wrap its long, snake-like body around John, his spiked suit of armour punctured its flesh. The beast could not get a hold of John, and as parts of the beast were being torn from it – dropping into the river and flowing away – John buried his sword deep into the head of the Lambton Worm, thus ending its reign of terror on Wearside. Tired and worn, John then made his way to the Lambton Estate whereupon he blew his hunting horn so that he could kill the family hound, but in a moment of foolish absent-mindedness and excitement, John's father ran out to congratulate him making himself the first living thing to be seen by his son after killing the beast. John could not bear the thought of killing his father, so when he noticed the hound padding across the courtyard towards him, he drew his sword and cut it down in its tracks, but it was too late; the Lambton family was cursed.

Of course, the tale of John Lambton and the Lambton Worm curse is well rooted in the 'folkloric' aspect of Wearside's wonderful and rich history, but, surely, it never *really* happened … did it? They do say legends and tales such as these have a certain amount of truth in their origins, but one has to ask just what that truth is – if any – in regards to this wonderful and magical tale of dragons and knights. We do know that a succession of the Lambton generations died before their time and with terrible and painful demises. Two of which died in battles, one at Wakefield and one at Marston Moor, another Lambton died early in life after he drowned, and another died in an accident involving a coach and horses … what you make of this is up to you, but I think it's certainly interesting and much food for thought.

The majority of the tales produced herein are drawn from a variety of different sources, with some tales being relatively new but most of them dating way back; heck, I have even included some of my own paranormal encounters experienced during my adventures in Wearside, and believe me when I say I have had some hair-raising encounters. I am willing to wager that a lot

An old line drawing illustrating 'Sunderland, Wearmouth Bridge over the River Wear'. (Courtesy of Newcastle Libraries and Information Service)

of the older tales included would have been more or less long forgotten by the good folk of Wearside today, if they were ever aware of them in the first place. It has been my 'mission', so to speak, to resurrect and breathe a new lease of life into these long-forgotten accounts of apparitions and tales of terror, and make them available to a whole new generation of Wearsiders. I have endeavoured to re-tell these accounts in their truest form and have avoided embellishment and sensationalism in order to keep them as original as they were when they were first told. It is my hope that these accounts will be kept and passed down to future generations.

The good folk of Wearside need to be aware of their wonderful haunted heritage, and it has been an absolute pleasure for me to be able to compile this book of their finest ghost tales. However, one has to bear in mind that this book barely even scratches the surface when it comes to documenting all of the ghost accounts of the county, and I can bet you a pound to a penny that for every story I have included in this book there will be a plethora of hitherto undiscovered ones just waiting to be found. Ghosts are everywhere – I have always maintained this stance and in light of this, there is sure to be many more tales to be told, each one personal to those that witness it.

All that remains to be said now, is that I hope you enjoy reading this book of hauntings as much as I have enjoyed researching and compiling it. Make yourself comfortable in your favourite armchair, dim the lights and, perhaps with a glass of whisky, prepare yourself for a fascinating journey through the wonderful county that is 'Haunted Wearside'.

Darren W. Ritson, 2013

1

HOUSES AND DWELLINGS

The Hendon Poltergeist

Being a known member of the Society for Psychical Research (SPR) due to my research, which includes the now famous South Shields Poltergeist case, I often get case referrals which are generally in, but not limited to, the north of England. Guy Lyon Playfair (of the Enfield Poltergeist fame) occasionally drops me a line to inform me of these 'interesting cases' that have either been in the news, or have been reported to the SPR, which I will then look into in the interests of the society, reporting my findings back to Guy. The following account of an alleged poltergeist is one of my many case referrals.

Strangely, a few days before I received the message from Guy, my attention was roused to the case by Mike Hallowell, with whom I had previously pursued the South Shields Poltergeist. Mike informed me of the paranormal activity that had been going on in the house on Toward Road in the Hendon area of Sunderland, and told me he had already visited the house on a number of occasions and had begun his task of accumulating the evidence in order to 'help' the distraught residents. Newcastle ghost walker and founder of Alone in the Dark Entertainment, Steve Taylor had originally informed Mike of the alleged haunting and said that he required his assistance. He too had received a telephone call from a distressed occupant of the house after a local medium had visited and openly admitted that he could not help.

In the early days of the 'infestation' (for that is what poltergeists do – infest), the occupant of the haunted abode, Marie Williams, had claimed that she had heard some footsteps making their way up the stairs in her house, even though she knew there was no one else around at the time. It was a month or so after she had moved into the three-storey house with her six children in 2011. Other paranormal things then occurred, such as apparitions manifesting within the house, which were seen by Marie and her children. They included a man dressed in trousers and a white shirt, and two phantom girls. Typical poltergeist-like symptoms soon followed: doors were being slammed closed when nobody was near them; objects were being thrown around the house and mysteriously being placed elsewhere by unseen hands; bedrooms were being completely overturned when no one was inside them; curtains being opened and closed on their own and the occupant of the house also reported being scratched by the so-called entity. After a while, Marie contacted a local 'psychic' called Sean Roper, who visited the house and claimed that the spirit energies were like nothing he had ever seen before. He claimed that the entity was so strong there was nothing he could do to help. Soon after, Mike Hallowell became involved in the case and this was shortly followed by a large piece in the *Sunderland Echo* on Wednesday, 7 March 2012.

This is where the case began to take an interesting, yet very unorthodox, turn. In the last few years, Mike has undergone a life-changing event, in the form of religious conversion to the Muslim faith. During the transition from his Native American spirituality to the Islamic way, he became very much aware of the Islamic/Middle Eastern conviction in the paranormal. The more he learned about what the Muslims call 'the unseen world' the more he craved knowledge about it – that is Mike all

over. Now, being an open-minded individual myself with the desire to learn more about any belief system of the paranormal, I was intrigued to hear what Mike was learning. After listening intently to Mike about what he had to say regarding the entity known as the Jinn, I decided to do some research of my own to find out just what these Islamic entities are. It was at this point that Mike told me that he believed the house in Hendon was haunted by Jinn (the word Jinn is singular as well as plural), and he had some quite compelling evidence to prove it.

A good investigator of the paranormal should not dismiss anything outright, neither should they accept things at face value, but study any available evidence for themselves to draw their own conclusions based upon it. Sadly, the studying of actual evidence very rarely seems to occur, although there are plenty of conclusions – usually erroneous – thrown around like confetti at a wedding! When one is confronted with evidence of something, evidence that is rather convincing, then you must go where the evidence takes you; and Mike's evidence suggested to me the potential presence of Jinn.

I asked Mike to sum up why he thought the house in Hendon was Jinn infested and he told me:

Regarding the 'Sunderland Jinn', we concluded that the entities in the house were indeed Jinn for a number of reasons, not least of which they

Toward Road in Hendon, Sunderland; the scene of a haunted laundry in 1891 and a poltergeist in 2012.

specifically said they were such in an EVP recording, but which we also heard in 'real time' with our own ears as it was being recorded. The behaviour of the entities contained several unique, Jinn-like features; language peculiarities, the 'gifting' of apports to the experients with specific cultural significance, masquerading as human beings, etc. Also, there was the presence of specific noises peculiar to the Jinn; the 'Jinn Whoop' – some say it is a call, similar to an animal howl - and the 'Jinn Cluck'.

In my subsequent quest looking into Jinn lore, the first thing I discovered was that the Jinn pre-date the Islamic faith and originated in Arabian folklore. Contrary to popular belief, they are *not* the genies from TV, old movies or pantomime that most folk may think they are, but real entities with physical (not

spiritual) bodies that are substantially different to ours and not normally visible to humans; and they will certainly not grant you three wishes. They were only integrated into Islamic mythology after the prophet Muhammad experienced Jinn first-hand in the seventh century, during the early stages of Islam. Created by Allah, Jinn are said to be creatures of free will made from smokeless fire, but can take the form of human beings or animals.

The Jinn are said to live alongside humanity, only in an alternate dimension and live normal lives just like humans do. Like humans, some Jinn are said to be good and some Jinn are said to be evil. It is said that the Jinn once occupied the living world that we live in now, but were banished by Allah after they turned corrupt and began to kill one another. Humans were then placed upon the earth.

Occasionally, Jinn can sometimes slip back through into our 'world' and cause mischief and mayhem, which some Muslims believe we interpret as 'poltergeist' activity. It is thought that the entire Jinn population are biding their time and are awaiting the right moment to retake the world they once called home – our present world. What once began as an Arabian/Middle Eastern folkloric belief is now a global phenomenon that millions of people worldwide believe in. Now, I am not about to recite the *Shahaddah* and convert to Islam, but I am prepared to give their beliefs and ideals in regards to the paranormal some serious thought.

Whether the entity residing at Hendon is a poltergeist or something completely different remains to be seen, but one thing is for sure, it is a fascinating case of the supernatural and I just wish I had the chance to get over there at that time and experience it for myself.

The Face in the Window

Numbers Garth, situated at the top of High St East in Sunderland city centre, was the setting for a macabre tale related to Alan Tedder by his friend Ernie Bewick who lived there as a lad. Alan then relayed the story to Mike Hallowell, who in turn relayed it to me.

Back in the 1930s, close to Berger's Pawnshop on the High Street, there was a narrow alleyway. By day, the alley looked pretty much like dozens of others that littered the centre of Sunderland, but at night it took on an eerie ambiance that deterred all but the residents from walking along its cobbled footpaths. One dwelling in particular was given a wide berth by children and adults alike, for it was said that a woman had been murdered there decades earlier. Her ghost, so the story went, still inhabited the building.

Sometimes the old house would stand empty for months or even years at a time, for its reputation deterred even those who were desperate for accommodation from moving in. Whenever anyone did occupy the premises, they never stayed long because, according to tradition, the ghost would drive them out. One day, in 1932, some passing children happened to look up at an upstairs window and, to their horror, saw the ghostly face of an old woman staring down at them through a cracked pane of glass. From that day forth until the house was demolished, no one dared to set foot inside.

The Sad Lady of Ford

There is a street in the heart of the Ford Estate that is the epicentre of one of the saddest ghost stories I have ever heard. Some years ago, a resident of the street (which for a number of reasons, I do not intend to name) told fellow researcher, Alan Tedder that they lived in a haunted house. At first nothing was seen, but household objects would

An artist's impression of the 'ghost face at the window' that was seen at Numbers Garth, Sunderland, back in 1932 by some passing children. (Courtesy of Julie Olley)

Who was the elderly woman, or more precisely, who had she been? When Mike Hallowell chatted with Alan about this story, he asked him a very pertinent question: 'Had she been left alone, ignored by neighbours and family, abandoned in a house which not only became her prison but also finally her tomb?'

It is impossible to say, of course. The woman may not even have lived in the street in question, but merely had a strong emotional attachment to that house for some reason. We can only hope that if she hasn't already done so, she soon finds the peace she seeks.

The Mystery Child of Town End Farm

move around without human intervention and the residents could 'sense a presence' of some kind.

After a while, the householders could also hear the sound of sobbing within the dwelling. Faint at first, it slowly but steadily became more pronounced. The general tenor of the voice indicated that it belonged to an elderly woman. It was said that the sounds were 'the most heart-rending, pitiful sobs' imaginable.

Seemingly, the tenant saw the apparition of the old lady only once. As suspected, she was old, stooped and had grey hair. What disturbed the witness, though, was her desperately sad appearance. She was just standing there, sobbing, as if completely heartbroken.

A dwelling in the Town End Farm estate is to have been haunted many years ago. The gist of the story is that the family who lived there vacated the premises briefly to go on holiday. However, when they returned a neighbour told them that she had seen a young boy staring out from one of the bedroom windows during their absence. Had they left their young son at home during their vacation? They had not and asserted that no one should have been in the dwelling at all during their absence.

Puzzled, the family simply got on with their lives and dismissed the incident, but not long afterwards strange things began to happen. A ball of light was seen moving across a bedroom before suddenly vanishing, and then items of jewellery began to disappear. The lady of the house was so puzzled that she enlisted the help of a local medium who agreed to investigate. She said that the house was haunted by a young boy who gazed out of the window looking for his sister. On learning of the missing jewellery, the medium told the lady to look behind a certain piece of furniture and, lo and behold, there it was.

The Green Street Ghost

Green Street was a bustling walkway in Sunderland that has long since been demolished, but at one time boasted a church, convent, shops and numerous tenements. In 1930, rumours flooded the area that a particular house in the street was haunted and local journalists did not take much time – or encouragement – to begin investigating what promised to be a very juicy story. It seems that the woman who lived in the house was extremely distressed because her daughter refused to stay on the premises due to the presence of what she called 'the goblin'.

Allegedly, the woman had lived in her rented tenement apartment for over a decade and nothing untoward had ever occurred there. However, after coming into some money, she purchased the building and that is when the trouble started. Two of the woman's sons shared a room on the top floor, and one evening they were 'horsing around'

when they heard the door handle rattle forcefully. Curious, they opened the door and looked out onto the landing but there was no one there. Their elder sister, a level-headed and strong-willed girl, treated their talk of a ghost with scorn, adding that she would happily go into the attic room on her own without even using a candle – big mistake. In fact, she didn't even manage to get inside the room before the ghost made its presence felt. As soon as she reached the landing, her brothers heard her scream for help. They dashed up the stairs and found her in a state of nervous collapse, claiming that a ghostly hand had touched her.

Later, whilst being interviewed by a local reporter, the woman was asked whether any pets were kept in the house or whether it was overrun with vermin. This, the journalist suggested, could well have been responsible for the noises. However, the woman said that this was impossible. Yes, there was a dog in the house, she admitted, but it had only been purchased by one of her sons *after* the phenomena had begun, and then only so he could train it to catch 'the goblin'! She also added that the only way an intruder – human, canine or other – could have reached the upper rooms was by the stairwell, at which point they would have been seen. In any case, on each occasion, a thorough search of the house was carried out and no intruder was found.

The effect upon the male children was quite profound – and decidedly unpleasant. The boys now refused categorically to stay in the attic room and slept on the floor below. On one occasion, an elderly woman had called at the dwelling and asked the owner if she had a vacant room to let. The family was so elated at the thought of the haunted room being occupied that they allowed her to live in it rent-free. However, one morning she came downstairs in an agitated manner and asked her landlady if the two sons had crept into her room during the night and pulled her bedclothes off, adding that she had heard the door to her room open. The owner told her that they had not and made the mistake of sharing with the new lodger some of the past ghostly shenanigans that had occurred in the room. The elderly woman was so discomfited that she packed her bags and immediately vacated the premises, never to be seen again.

The puppy that was purchased to catch 'the goblin' was also to be tested one night. The family members were all downstairs, save for the husband who was asleep in bed. The dog had been placed in the haunted room to see if it could precipitate a reaction from the ghost. At some point, the woman heard footsteps coming down the stairs. Thinking that it was her husband, she shouted, 'When you go back upstairs, knock on the door of the room with the dog in and see if it will bark!' She received no answer. She shouted her request a second time, but there was only a hushed silence. Puzzled, she opened the parlour door and found no one there. She ascended the stairs

to her bedroom where she found her spouse in bed sleeping soundly. Alarmed, she woke her husband from his slumber and told him about the footsteps on the stairs. Both made a thorough search, but found no one.

The sister of the lady of the house had recently married and when they came to visit, they stayed in the attic room. The couple were warned about the paranormal antics, but the sister simply laughed and dismissed such talk as nonsense. Her husband – seemingly a decent chap, but not of rigorous disposition – suddenly decided that they should depart sharpish and head back to Hartlepool. His wife would have none of it, however. As things turned out, her foolish bravado was promptly replaced with naked fear. On the very first night, while awake in bed, she heard the latch of the bedroom door rattle, followed by a loud, repetitive thumping sound. No longer as brave as before, she quickly roused her husband and they both listened to the horrendous din with open-mouthed surprise. Not only could they hear the booming thumps now, but also the sound of sticks being chopped.

Inevitably, people began to ask whether a tragedy had ever occurred in the house. The woman said that she had never heard of any, but could recall one story she had been told shortly after she had moved in. During the Second World War, two soldiers had been billeted in the house and had been asked to sleep in the haunted room. Neither had subsequently reported anything happening in the room itself, but both had seen the ghost of an old woman hovering on the landing outside.

By the time all of these incredible stories made the headlines, of course, almost all of Sunderland was aware of the Green Street Ghost. However, things became even more dramatic when a second resident stepped forward and claimed that her house was haunted too. She explained that she had rented her own attic room to an elderly gentleman and one morning, at six o'clock, he happened to look down at the back door of the premises and there he saw 'the ghost of an old woman' in the yard. The spectre turned and stared at him before vanishing.

This was all it took to elevate the story into a social crisis. Thousands of onlookers poured into Green Street to catch a glimpse of the ghost, the old woman or indeed any of the sundry other apparitions, which had now been added to the list. One resident became so irate that she threw a bucket of water over them in a desperate effort to get the crowd to disperse. But still they came, many rapping on windows to ask which was the haunted house, while the more boisterous boasted that for a bet they would even spend a night in it. By now, of course, they had several houses from which to choose.

One prosaic explanation was that the eerie sounds were being made by trains passing through a nearby tunnel, although this would not account for the apparitions that were seen by numerous witnesses. There was one incident that had occurred in Green Street that just might have had some bearing on the haunting, although it is a long shot. On 11 July 1900, the female resident of 30 Green Street had been out for the evening. On returning home, she opened a cupboard, reached inside and removed a bottle of whisky. Or rather, she removed a bottle that had a whisky label on it. Unfortunately, someone had replaced the whisky with ammonia. She removed the cork and took a large swig, thereafter falling to the floor in agony clutching her throat, which felt as if it was on fire. The poor woman died. Could it have been her ghost that frequented Green Street? Maybe, but the street has gone now and so, presumably, have 'the goblins', or ghosts.

The Ghost Who Searched for Annie

Here is another story that comes directly from Mike Hallowell's archives, published verbatim with his kind permission.

Northumberland Street ran eastwards away from Crowtree Road, and was a quite unremarkable residential block; until February, 1932, that is, when the lady at number 53, a tenement, revealed that her dwelling was haunted by a ghost who seemed to have a wooden leg. Mrs Clinton – for it was she – was the resident who first brought the tale to the ears of the general public, for she stated that most evenings between 11.30 p.m. and midnight the ghost would go up and down the communal stairs, also banging on the walls. The eerie footfalls sounded as if they were being made by a man with a wooden leg.

Initially the strange noises were put down to cats but then Mrs Clinton went to the back yard tap to fill a bucket with water, and was startled to see a man in an overcoat. Although we aren't told what, there must have been something spectral about him as the householder promptly went dashing back inside. Mrs Clinton was a devout Roman Catholic, and seemingly did not believe in apparitions, but as the paranormal phenomena increased and started to impinge upon her sleep, she decided that drastic measures were called for and called upon the services of a local spiritualist medium. She was supported in this venture by her neighbour, John Roper, who had also had one or two brushes with the phantasm.

Roper's daughter was in hospital at the time, and his wife had gone to visit the child. Later in the evening he heard the sound of footsteps coming up the tenement stairs and, presuming that his wife had returned, opened the door to let her in. His wife wasn't there, however, and not a soul was to be seen. Later, Roper recalled that the footsteps he'd heard were different to those experienced by Mrs Clinton. Whereas she'd heard the sound of a man with a wooden leg, the footfalls he'd heard had seemed completely normal.

The following Sunday the medium arrived and promptly struck up a rapport with the ghost on the stairs. The spirit revealed that in life he had been called John Henry Turner and had committed suicide after being unjustly accused of some vile crime that he had not actually committed. Turner said that he was seeking 'eternal peace', but could only do so if his name was cleared. To do this he needed to get in touch with someone called Annie and, presumably, wanted to enlist the medium's help in doing this.

The medium told Mrs Clinton that he would return two days hence with some other spiritualist colleagues to take matters further. Things took a strange twist when a chap from Grangetown informed Mrs Clinton and Mr Roper that he had actually known 'Annie', and even had a photograph of her. Annie, he said, had been orphaned at an early age and died when she was just 17. Eventually the case faded from the headlines and little more was said about it. However, a neighbour further down the street did say that during World War I she had actually lived at 53 Northumberland Street and had often heard the same, eerie thudding sound on the stairwell accompanied by 'the sound of a panel being raised then dropped'.

It seems that the ghost of John Henry Turner never found Annie and one presumes that the ghost still haunts the area because he could not leave until Annie cleared his name.

The Chester Terrace Window Smasher

In March 1966, a curious set of circumstances arose in Chester Terrace, Sunderland – near Trimdon Street – when residents suddenly found their windows being broken with wild abandon. Despite the frequency of the attacks, the police were unable to catch the perpetrator, which in turn led to householders claiming that a poltergeist was at work.

Both by night and by day, the invisible assailant repeatedly shattered windows in the street, and some rather more sceptically minded folk suggested an explanation far less exotic than the presence of a poltergeist – unruly young children. Could youngsters have repeatedly smashed windows on an almost nightly basis without being apprehended? The idea was dismissed when it was pointed out that some of the missiles used to break the windows, such as lumps of concrete, were so heavy that it would have been impossible for a child to lift them.

Eventually, the police instigated special patrols of the neighbourhood involving officers with dogs. Perhaps the sight of a mean-looking canine might deter whoever was responsible? Not quite. As one officer stood talking to a group of men in a back lane, a milk bottle flew over a yard wall, narrowly missing them and exploding at their feet. They rushed into the yard in question, only to find it deserted.

Even the fire brigade got in on the act, setting up a searchlight designed to illuminate the area and thus deter the perpetrator.

On one occasion, milk bottles were thrown near a local dairy; the police cordoned off the area around the premises and were convinced that no one could escape from the boundaries. Highly trained police dogs were let loose inside, but the building was completely empty. Such baffling incidents did seem to make it less likely by the day that the vandalism involved any sort of human agency. As Sunderland researcher Alan Tedder himself questioned, 'How could a human have tempted a speedy arrest by such crass acts, or how could a human have been such a clot as to throw milk bottles from a dairy yet elude arrest when the police threw a cordon round the building and trained dogs were let loose inside to flush out the culprit?'

Several days later, an arrest was made when a local man was caught throwing a steel bolt. As Tedder admitted, the problem was that 'the bolt was a missile so out of context with the others that one was forced to reach the conclusion that this fellow was merely aping the event'. At court, he was charged with a list of eleven offences, yet only two could be proven against him, for a local vicar testified at court that the defendant had been in his company when many of the alleged crimes had taken place. Was a poltergeist at work, then? Perhaps, and if it was I would not expect an arrest any time soon.

Chester Terrace, Sunderland, where in 1966 a spate of 'paranormal' window smashing took place.

The Clicking Ghost of Farringdon

In September 1976, the tenants of two adjoining flats in Farringdon discovered simultaneously that their dwellings were haunted. The house-holders noticed that objects were being moved around, seemingly without human intervention. Keys would be placed on a table, only for them to be found later on top of the toilet cistern, and pints of milk that had been in a refrigerator would disappear, only to be found later in a wardrobe.

Within weeks, both families started to see fleeting shadows in their homes. The children in both abodes claimed that they were being stalked by a 'shadow man' with 'evil eyes'. They were so frightened that they enlisted the help of a priest who attempted to rectify the situation, but to no avail.

The priest carried out a blessing at both flats and for a while things seemed to calm down. After about two weeks, the phenomena returned worse than ever, as is often the case. Objects were hurled across the lounge with terrific force, doors opened and slammed shut of their own accord, the gas ovens in the kitchen would turn themselves on and light switches would be activated. Through all of this, both families could do nothing but watch in bemusement and fear.

The bizarre aspect of this case was that the appearance of the entity – or at least, the manifestation of its presence – was usually accompanied by weird clicking sounds that had no obvious origin. Over the succeeding weeks, the phenomena intensified. Jewellery started to go missing and payment books were found on top of a bath-room cabinet, standing on end in a row, like Christmas cards. The woman of one of the dwellings then caught sight of the 'shadow man' standing by her son's bed. She screamed, after which the entity simply turned, walked away and disappeared.

In the adjoining flat, the residents once again called upon the priest for help, but as soon as he left the residence it filled with what was described as, 'an awful stench of burning'. Eventually, news of the case reached the ears of a couple from Darlington who were actively involved in investigating the supernatural. They visited the house but, to my knowledge, were unable to make any progress. A team of psychical researchers from Lancashire spent two nights in both flats and sealed off every door in the house with tape. During the night, the doors flew open even though they had been taped shut. The team also noticed the horrible burning smell that had first manifested itself after the visit of the priest. The investigators were convinced that neither family had been involved in any form of trickery or deception. Inevitably, both tenants requested a move in due course.

Betting Tom of Hedworth Street

During the Second World War, there was a dwelling occupied by a family who conscientiously followed the instructions from the War Office about observing blackout protocols and regulations.

The lady of the house dutifully climbed upon a table to pin a black-out curtain at the window and after fixing it securely in place, she stepped back, fully intending to step down onto a chair and then onto the floor. However, as her foot took its first step back on the table, she heard a peculiar crunching sound, as though her heel had shattered something. On turning around to see what she had stepped on, she was alarmed to find an elderly gentleman sitting upon the chair! Speechless, she gazed at him as he carefully filled out a betting slip with a wax crayon. It later transpired that the man, identified as 'Tom', had lived in the house many years previously. Sadly, he had switched on his gas fire but had forgotten to ignite it, so when he fell asleep he was gassed to death in the chair where he slumbered.

One could assume that when the woman stepped back she put her foot down upon one of Tom's wax crayons and broke it. How anyone could break a ghostly crayon with a flesh-and-blood foot is anybody's guess, but still, that is why we call things like this paranormal.

The Fatfield Girl

A row of cottages once stood in Fatfield and were inhabited by staff of the well-known Lambton Lion Park. One evening in summer many years ago, three employees, who also happened to be friends, were sitting in one of the cottages when, at 11 p.m., the volume on the TV set turned to maximum. Then, just as quickly, it fell silent. At the same time, the room temperature dropped dramatically and a strange whistling noise could be heard.

Also in the room at that time was a dog that began to behave in an extremely agitated manner and barked loudly. A previous owner of the cottage had also experienced some bizarre phenomena there. One evening, just as he left the cottage, he happened to glance at an upstairs window and saw a young girl staring down at him. The man's daughter became so afraid that she decided to leave the property. As she walked through the front door, a photograph of her hanging in the hall fell from the wall and jumped onto the fourth step of the stairwell. Curiously, visitors had often recalled that as soon as they placed a foot upon that very step an icy chill overcame them.

The Ghost Lady of Middle Herrington

A woman by the name of Smith once lived in the old mansion house at Middle Herrington. The woman was commonly known to her neighbours as 'Lady Peat', and throughout the area was known for her penny pinching ways. Lady Peat was, I was told, despised by the shopkeepers of Herrington and Sunderland. Their loathing stemmed from the fact that, despite her considerable wealth, she repeatedly stole food from local stores instead of paying for it. One exasperated trader had a brainwave and determined that the next time Lady Peat entered the premises he would put his plan into action.

Several days later, the old woman came into the shop and, bold as brass, picked up a large slab of butter and hid it under her clothing. The shopkeeper asked Lady Peat to accompany him into the rear of the store where a roaring fire was burning. He then chatted to her amicably and managed to keep her there long enough for the butter to melt. He only allowed Lady Peat to leave when the melted butter was trickling down her legs. It is thought by some folk that Lady Peat's ghost continued to haunt the locality for years after her death but as we shall now see, there is another spectral lady of Middle Herrington.

Her name was Isabella Young, who just happened to be the maid to the aforementioned Lady Peat. Isabella was cruelly murdered in 1815, and to this day the murder remains unsolved. Lady Peat had left Herrington House in order to collect rent and had left Isabella on her own. Isabella did not like being in the house on her own and had recently complained about hearing certain noises and disturbances, as though an intruder was attempting to gain access while she was left 'home alone'. She had asked someone to spend the night with her, but they refused and the most they would do was see her home safely and watch her enter the house, locking the doors behind her.

A rare photograph of Herrington House (or Herrington Hall). Sadly, the house has been confined to the realms of history after a fire raised it to the ground in August 1815. (Courtesy of England's Lost Country Houses)

In the early hours of August 1815, the local blacksmith, John Stonehouse, looked out from his lodging windows to see Herrington House on fire and burning furiously. Knowing Isabella was alone inside the house, he roused his brother and the pair dashed over to rescue her. After eventually finding his way into the house, he realised it was too late and that Isabella was dead. However, it was not the fire nor the smoke that killed the young maid, but an intruder inside the house, for she was found with a broken jaw, a battered and caved-in head and, chillingly, her eyes had been pushed back into their sockets.

Shortly afterwards, three men – James Wolf, his son George and another chap, John Eden – were arrested and subsequently charged with Young's murder. All three strenuously protested their innocence, but were charged with burglary, murder and arson. The authorities took so long to prosecute that the case was eventually taken over by the Society of Friends. In no time at all they found new evidence that completely proved the men's innocence and they were, therefore, pardoned and subsequently released, leaving the brutal murder unsolved. It is for this reason that some local folk in Middle Herrington believe that the area is haunted by the murdered maid.

Her ghost, which is thought to have no eyes, is said to be seen in and around Herrington Park, scurrying through the trees and pathways with her arms stretched out in front of her as she blindly tries to figure out where she is. Other sightings of ghostly women have also been reported in Herrington Park as stated earlier, which is close to where Herrington House once stood. This spectre is

The empty field where Herrington House once stood.

A closer shot of the stone stairs; the only remaining part of Herrington House. Note stone stairwell on the image on page 26.

Middle Herrington Park.

assumed to be that of Lady Peat. In the park there is a stone sculpture that takes the shape of a pile of coins with an inscription on it. This small monument commemorates the story of Lady Peat, the miser of Herrington, and commemorates the death of her maid, Isabella Young.

Above *The stone sculpture that takes the shape of a pile of coins with an inscription on it.*

Right *A circular plaque displaying information regarding the unsolved murder of Isabella Young and indicating the site of Herrington House.*

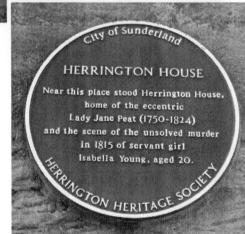

2

PUBS, INNS AND TAVERNS

The Jolly Sailor Pub

The Jolly Sailor public house is located on East Street, which is the main road between South Shields and the city of Sunderland. It is a former coaching inn from the eighteenth century. Michael Hallowell's book, *Ales and Spirits: The Haunted Pubs and Inns of South Tyneside*, talks about the Jolly Sailor. He says:

> When you walk in via the side entrance, you immediately become isolated from the traffic and other unwelcome signs of life in the 21st century, and are plunged into a quaint old world of yesterday. When you enter the Jolly Sailor, the past greets you like a warm breeze.

I couldn't agree more – when I entered the building one night to chat to the staff (via the same side entrance that Mike talks about) it was literally like a step back in time. On the right-hand side there are stairs leading up to the next level and on the right of there, halfway down the corridor, is the snug bar complete with oak beams across the ceiling with all sorts of memorabilia from the past hanging from them. Old-fashioned photographs and paintings festoon the walls, the red and orange lights dimly light the room and the huge, roaring open fire burns furiously, creating a fabulous resonance of times gone by.

The Jolly Sailor is one of the north east's more famous haunted inns and it was a real pleasure to be sitting in the 'snug' area chatting to the staff about their ghosts. I first spoke to manageress Beverley Jackson, who informed me that on one occasion while at the pub alone, she was in the kitchen getting on with her duties when suddenly she heard the fridge door open. She told me that when she glanced up she saw the door open and to her surprise, there was a man's hand holding the door from behind it. What was odd about this was that she could see no legs where a pair of legs should have been. As she watched, the fridge door closed and no man was to be seen anywhere.

She then informed me of another encounter in the pub that she experienced on the next floor up. 'It appears that there is a playful ghost who likes to toy around with people's possessions,' she told me. Getting ready to leave the pub one day, she was putting on her coat and had a large bunch of keys in her hand. She put the keys down for one moment to put her arms in the sleeves and when she went to pick her keys up, they were gone. She searched the room high and low, and just to be certain she searched the rest of the building, although she knew for sure that she had just that minute placed the keys down. She then asked a friend, who was downstairs at the time, to help her locate these keys and they both then searched the inn high and low to no avail. The two women were just about to give up their search when they glanced down and noticed that the keys were back in the exact place she had originally left them before putting on her coat. She is adamant that they were not there during the original search and is convinced that the mischievous ghost that lurks within this old boozer is responsible.

The pub is also famous for having an apparition known as 'The Green Lady', who has been seen on occasion wondering around the upper levels of the inn wearing a long, green, flowing dress, hence the name Green Lady. She is believed to be a woman who once lived at the inn and was rumoured to have been courting a coach driver from

The Jolly Sailor pub in Whitburn. Probably the most well-known haunted pub in Wearside. It is reputedly haunted by 'The Green Lady', and a playful ghost that likes to move around personal belongings.

Newcastle-upon-Tyne. She had big plans for her future with her lover until one day he abandoned her for another lady. This, of course, devastated her and legend has it, riddled with pain and sheer anguish, she locked herself in her room and subsequently starved herself to death.

The manageress told me of an experience she had one night while working in the main bar. She was standing behind the counter and chatting to three of her regulars at last orders. The rest of the bar had been vacated and as these three regulars were friends of hers, she locked the doors and let them stay just a little longer to finish their drinks. Before coming back to the bar, she made sure no one else was still inside the pub, then went back to her friends and continued with her conversation.

The three friends finished their drinks and as she was about to let them out she suddenly saw a figure drift past the door and along the adjoining corridor. 'It happened so quickly', she said. Her first thought was that she must

The village sign of Whitburn.

have had another customer whom she had forgotten all about or perhaps missed when emptying the pub at last orders. That was until she walked into the corridor to greet this person only to find no one was there. She looked in the lavatories, in the snug, and all around the pub, but could find no one except her three friends who were in the bar all the time. 'Must just be another of the Jolly Sailor's ghosts,' she said.

The Golden Lion Pub/Hotel

One of the most exciting venues I have ever had the privilege to spend the night in searching for ghosts has to be, without question, the Golden Lion Pub in Seaham. The pub is one of Seaham's oldest drinking dens and dates back a few hundred years, although I am not sure exactly how many. Out of general interest, it is rumoured that Albert Pierrepoint (the well-known executioner of over 400 men and women, including Britain's last condemned inmate, Ruth Ellis) stayed there on a regular basis while he was 'up north on his business'. Speaking with the pubs owner, I ascertained the information that the building had been a school of sorts, where children had various lessons and spent much of their time. After a number of ghostly children had been reportedly seen there, subsequent enquiries showed this to be the case. Apart from that, very little is known about the history of this particular pub.

The Golden Lion in Seaham; haunted by a violent glass-smashing entity that scared the living daylights out of the author and his colleagues during a number of overnight investigations there.

The pubs proprietor said to me, 'There is just something about this old building ... it terrifies me and I hate being the last one in at night and having to lock up by myself.' The proprietor has a friend who claims to hold mediumistic abilities and I had a chance to meet him during one of my visits there. He told me:

I have visited the Golden Lion on a number of occasions and have frequently picked up on the presence of two spirit children. They run around and play in the upper corridors of the pub. They are brother and sister with one being older and taller than the other [a pretty common facet amongst most siblings if you ask me]. One spectral child has a neck injury due to falling down a flight of stairs so this could be the result of this child's untimely death. There is a ghost of a male adult too. He is believed to be a teacher, perhaps, or at least someone who had authority over the children at the school.

During a number of investigations into the Golden Lion, myself and a few certain individuals were very fortunate to have experienced some very strange paranormal phenomena indeed. Most of this bewildering activity was witnessed and can be verified by a number of the people who were there on the nights in question. Thankfully, we also managed to capture some of it on camera and on video tape too. During the early stages of one of our first investigations at the public house, we conducted a séance in one of the rooms of the upper levels. During this séance, a number of things occurred, for which we can find no explanation. For example, not long after the experiment began from out of the darkness and the deathly silence we all heard a crystal-clear, long, guttural breath that would have sent shivers down the spines of most. The harrowing sound of a child laughing was also heard, along with that of a more melancholic sound of a woman sobbing; we can say with 100 per cent certainty that the noises we heard came from within the building. It was nerve-racking yet very exciting to say the least and our hearts were racing, our hands were sweating, and, to this day, no explanation could be (or has been) found for these anomalous noises.

Later that evening, one of the most peculiar photographs I have ever seen was taken. As I was investigating an area known as 'the pit' (an opened cellar area of the pub, which had been turned into a dance floor) I suddenly became a little anxious, and for seemingly no reason, the temperature sharply and unexpectedly plummeted. I felt a little panic-stricken and nervous, so I proceeded to take an impromptu photograph or two and caught one of the most amazing mist anomaly pictures that I have ever seen. I might also add that I saw this mist with my naked eye when the flashgun went off. I was lucky to catch it on camera. It must now be emphasised that I held the camera out at arm's length and refrained from breathing until I had taken the photo, due to the 'breath factor' (where breathing out can cause vapour to materialise in front of the lens and flash, resulting in something that seems to be a ghostly mist appear on the photograph). This is a practice that most ghost hunters should adhere to during often cold and damp, overnight investigations.

Looking at this incredible photograph from a sceptic's view, one could suggest it might simply be cigarette smoke. This is not true, I can assure you, as no one was smoking on the investigation; not only that, but I was the only one down in the pit at that time and I was certainly not smoking. Smoking, for the record, is strictly forbidden while in these vigil conditions for this exact reason. Of course, you only have my word for this, don't you? When one looks at the mist itself, it is clear that it has a facial contour, as if I had caught the spirit or ghost as it was walking in front of me. However, 'pareidolia' springs to mind and cannot be ignored. Many pictures of alleged ghosts in windows or even faces in fogs and mists are simply patterns in the image that look like faces and certain shapes. Patterns in wallpaper and in curtains, when viewed at night, provide exactly the same sort of effect. It is thought that the first things the brain will look for, and register in such instances, are human faces. I am not saying that this picture is of a ghost with a face, I am merely pointing out it that it certainly looks like it. That aside, the mist is still considered anomalous and cannot be explained by any normal means.

We returned to the pub for another investigation on 26 September 2008, to carry on with our work. Fire had sadly torn through half the pub since

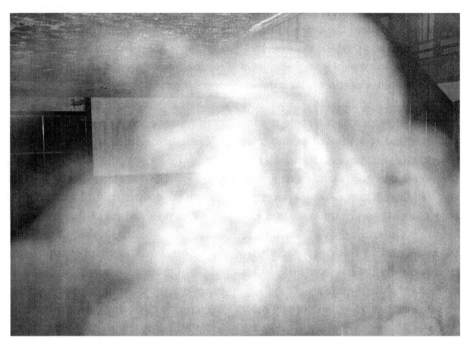

The area in the Golden Lion known as 'the pit' showing the amazing anomalous mist that was seen with the naked eye at the time of being caught on camera.

The same area in the Golden Lion taken seconds after the mist anomaly image was taken. As you can see, nothing is shown and all traces of the mist have gone.

our first visit leaving it in a terrible state of disrepair, so it was, therefore, now disused and derelict. The pub was a former shadow of itself with all electricity supplies being recently cut off. It was a dark and foreboding place and, to be quite honest, it was quite dangerous too. From around the beginning of 2007 the pub was completely abandoned by the owners, although they kept ownership of the property. Battered by the north-east winds and howling storms that come in from the ice-cold North Sea, the pub stood corroding and dilapidated. It was literally rotting on the spot.

That night, too, proved to be another night we would not forget in a hurry, with a number of terribly frightening things being observed by all that were there. The most harrowing incident occurred moments after we began to make our way to our observation posts, or vigil locations. A team member and I were heading off upstairs to investigate the upper floors of the inn, while two of the other team members were staying on the ground level to investigate the 'snug' area. As the other two investigators went into the snug, we pulled the door firmly closed behind us and began to make our way up the eerie, dark steps that led to the first floor. As we got a third of the way up the stairs we all heard a terrific crash, as though a glass or perhaps a light bulb had smashed on the floor. This came from inside the main bar area where nobody was situated at that point. Some choice language left our lips as

we both got one hell of a fright, at the same time we looked at each other in utter astonishment. We wondered what on earth this noise was.

As we made our way back down the stairs to investigate the noise, the other two investigators came out from the snug room door to explore; they had heard it too. We then made our way into the main bar area because this was clearly where the sound had come from and we found absolutely nothing out of place. We checked all the windows from outside to see if local vandals had decided to throw bricks through them and found they were all intact, or at least they were in the same condition as they were when we entered the building earlier on that evening. Besides, there was also nobody around outside and the streets were deathly quiet. Every effort was made to find a natural source of the breaking glass, but none was found. In fact, we couldn't even find any broken glass anywhere in that room, which added further intrigue to the already mysterious event. After scratching our heads and failing to come to a sensible working scenario about what could have made the noise, we then noticed a number of other odd things. The [unused] fridge door was found to be closed after we had left it open earlier on, and a trigger object of a cross that we had placed on the bar was found to have been moved. A certain degree of controlled pandemonium once again ensued and efforts were made to work out what could have happened. These incidents shook all of us, and to this day we have no idea what it was.

In a third investigation held there a few months later, the same phenomenon was experienced yet again with another glass exploding (either that or it was thrown by something). This incident – at least the auditory – was recorded on video tape and on EVP machines too. People may mock and say this is all made up, but I am telling you the truth. This was one of the most frightening nights I have ever had in a haunted pub and let me tell you why: if there was a ghost or an angry spirit inside that pub that likes to throw around pint pots or break glasses, then in all likelihood it knew we were in there with it. What was to stop this entity throwing the glass at any of the investigators? Nothing at all! And judging by the noise of the glass breaking, it must have thrown it bloody hard and with some brute force.

We attempted to roll a few pint pots off the bar to see if they could have smashed after accidentally rolling off the counter (the thought also crossed our minds), but they would not break and, besides, the pint pots were all standing up, so the 'rolling off the bar' theory would have been an unlikely event. Even after we threw them onto the hard floor, the pint pots would not smash! (Bear in mind this is not our usual practice when we visit pubs; the pub was old and derelict and the beer glasses were all destined to be binned, and any mess made would most certainly have been cleaned up.) We think they may have been strengthened somehow by the heat of the fire that tore through the building; all of the glasses were black and charred. You can now imagine how much power it would have taken for an entity to smash a glass if it had chosen to throw it across the room. Had it hit one of us instead of smashing in the bar, I think it is safe to assume that whoever it hit would have most certainly been seriously injured, or even killed – especially if it had hit one of us on the head.

This incident has given me a deeper respect for the paranormal. To be quite honest, after that occurrence, I would have been quite happy to leave the premises there and then, but we stayed a few more hours and finished the investigation. I must admit, after hundreds of overnight investigations in locations right across the UK, I have never felt so relieved to get out of a haunted venue when the night was over and when the sun was beginning to come up.

Blacksmith's Table, Washington

The Blacksmith's Table restaurant sits in the centre of Washington Village. It is a small, but old-world building steeped in history. The structure is over 400 years old and was originally the local blacksmith's workshop. Now it is a privately owned restaurant and is reputedly haunted by a number of ghosts and spectres.

On a visit to Washington Old Hall in 2003, I walked past the Blacksmith's Table and saw the owner, Paul, outside the premises. I had seen the restaurant on a video about north-east ghosts and recognised him immediately. I subsequently approached him and asked him all about the smithy's ghosts. He very kindly invited me inside for a cup of tea and proceeded to enlighten me about the wonderful spectres of the Blacksmith's Table. The first ghost he mentioned was that of the infamous highwayman, Robert Hazlitt.

In and around the areas of Long Bank, Wrekenton and Washington, I was told, a certain Robert Hazlitt 'worked the roads' as a notorious highwayman. He was an evil sort, so they say, and took no mercy on his terrified victims. After robbing a coach-and-four one day, he made off into the distance with his loot, but failed to realise that he was being watched by a sharp-eyed little local boy. Walking past the smithy one day, the boy happened to glance inside and see something. What he saw puzzled him somewhat, because it was a horse. He knew he had seen this horse somewhere before but could not think where, and then it hit him; this was the horse he had seen galloping off from the coach robbery only a few days earlier. Being a good sort, the

The Blacksmiths Table in Washington village is said to be haunted by at least a dozen ghosts and apparitions including the infamous highwayman, Robert Hazlitt.

The Old Hall Smithy sign standing outside the old blacksmith's workshop.

It is said that his corpse was brought back to the areas where he worked and hung up in a gibbet cage in the area then known as Gateshead Fell, as a deterrent to other would-be robbers.

It comes as no surprise, then, that his unquiet spirit is said to frequent the bar area of the actual restaurant and has reputedly been seen on many occasions by visitors to the restaurant, and many more times by the building's owners, Paul and Pam.

Other ghosts at the Blacksmith's Table include the blacksmith himself. He sits at a table in the restaurant and just watches the world go by. Seen on many occasions, this ghost disappears into thin air moments after being noticed. A spectral woman has also

boy dashed off and ran for miles to the nearest law enforcer, and subsequently informed him of the whereabouts of the highwayman's trusty steed.

The authorities rushed back to the smithy and asked the blacksmith if they could hide in the back shop and wait for Hazlitt to return for his horse. This was the best chance they had been given to apprehend him and they were not going to let him slip away. The blacksmith agreed to the plot and so the relevant authorities took their places in the workshop. This is where the main restaurant area is now. When Hazlitt turned up for his horse, he was subsequently captured. As he was apprehended and taken away, he was heard to lay a curse upon the blacksmith for Hazlitt knew what fate awaited him. Within a week, Hazlitt was hanged.

An artist's impression of Robert Hazlitt galloping along the old dirt tracks and trails that once festooned the areas of Long Bank, Wrekenton and Washington. (Courtesy of Julie Olley)

been seen materialising in the restaurant area. She then walks down the aisle and past the tables, turns right, and then walks straight through the wall and out into the main road. There is also the unknown ghost of a man that has been seen standing facing the wall in between the windows on the right-hand side as you walk into the building, near to the main entrance. He does not move at all, but eerily looks over his left shoulder. Paul once told me that they had even tried mediums to contact the other ghosts in the building, to see if they knew who he was.

Many other folk can bear witness to the plethora of ghosts that are said to reside at the Blacksmith's Table after seeing them whilst dining there. I asked Paul on one occasion just how many of the ghosts he had seen and he simply replied, 'All of them'.

3

ROADS AND STREETS

Sunderland to Newcastle Road – Headless Horseman

Back in the 1700s, the Boldons in nearby South Tyneside were just small villages, and what is now the A184 was, in most parts, little more than a country lane. Trees were far more populous then and driving a carriage along it at night in their shadow could be an eerie experience. To make matters worse, a highwayman frequented the area, constantly harassing his victims to 'stand and deliver'. The locals were enraged and set a trap. The ne'er-do-well was duly caught and tried at the assizes. The judge, with due solemnity, pronounced that his neck would be stretched at the gallows.

The vagabond's meeting with 'Old Ropey' may have put an end to his reign of robbery, but it did not stop him appearing. From time to time, reports are made of a headless horseman riding along the Sunderland to Newcastle road. I was informed by Mike Hallowell that similar stories were told further along the A184 at Sunderland, particularly near the recently restored old windmill, which stands near The Grange public house.

The horseman is always seen riding away from Sunderland and towards Newcastle – in the direction of Laverick Hall. A former publican, who ran one of the several public houses which line the A184, told Mike that he had never seen the horseman but he had, late at night, heard the horse's hooves as it galloped along.

The Spectre of Zetland Street

In his book, *Haunted Sunderland* (The History Press, 2008), Rupert Matthews has a small section dedicated to the Victorian man of Zetland Street. He states that during the compilation of his book, he was informed of a 'right posh ghost that wears a

Fulwell Mill in Fulwell, close to the spot where a headless horseman rides on Halloween.

The stretch of Sunderland Road near to the Grange Public House where a ghostly headless horseman has been seen and heard galloping.

Zetland Street, Sunderland.

drew the image of a well-dressed gentleman wearing Victorian garb.

Funnily enough, when I was in the Zetland Street area taking photographs for this book, I managed to chat with a few of the local folk and discussed 'the spectre' too. You would be surprised at how many of the older generation remember him and what I found out was rather interesting to say the very least. When I mentioned the idea that this chap was an alleged 'ghost', a look of perplexity quickly spread across the faces of those that I voiced it to, as if to say, 'Ghost? I never knew about a ghost.' One local went as far as saying, 'Yes, I saw him all the time as a youngster but he was a real flesh and blood person, not a ghost'. Another local, a woman this time, told me that he was indeed a real-life individual and was known locally and by everyone as 'the spectre' simply because he looked like an old-fashioned ghost dressed in his Victorian attire, but phantom he was not.

It quickly became clear to me that 'the spectre' who had been seen all those years ago and by all those people in the Zetland Street area was in actual fact an eccentric local that simply dressed in old-style clothes and a top hat, although why he dressed this way no one could tell me. I suggest to you the reader that over the years the story of the eccentric individual has become muddled and distorted, culminating in a real-life flesh and blood human – albeit an unconventional one – being slowly transformed into a Wearside ghost legend.

really smart suit' that frequented this section of town. Apparently, this spectral visitor has not been seen for a good while now, but at the time he was reported to just amble around the street aimlessly until he spotted somebody, anybody. Then, he would approach the individual as if he was going to ask them a question. Suddenly, and without warning, he would then vanish into thin air right in front of them.

How does Rupert know this man is a Victorian then? Well, during his research he got chatting to an old local man that could remember the tale well. He said, 'Back in the day, it was all the talk, and most folk these days won't have heard of him.' When asked if he could describe the ghost, the old chap said he could go one better and draw him. Using Rupert's paper and pen, he

However, until I can be certain of this I shall refrain from pouring cold water on this case and leave you with the thought that there may be a possibility that 'the spectre' has been seen after his real death, possibly by those that were unaware of his demise, therefore, mistaking the actual ghost for a live human. However, in Matthews's book he claims that after approaching people, 'the spectre' would 'vanish into thin air'. This could be a tad harder to explain away, assuming the 'vanishing into thin air' aspect of the sightings was not made up by some of those that claimed to have seen him of course! Also, the telling of ghost stories can be altered and embellished over many years, so this could be where the vanishing aspect comes from.

No one, however, during my visit there that day back in October 2012, could tell me who he actually was or when he actually died. I can safely assume that it was many years ago now and details such as these could also have been lost in the sands of time. So, if there is indeed anyone that knows the facts regarding this tale, please do get in touch, as I really would love to get to the bottom of this one. Who was he? When did he die? And, more importantly, when was the last reported sighting of 'the spectre'? If it was after his death, then maybe we are on to something.

The Ghost Nuns of Franklin Street

Back in the 1940s, on Franklin Street, just off Hylton Road in Sunderland, lived a widow and one of her daugh-

Franklin Street in Sunderland; a house on this street was once reported to have been haunted by the three nuns.

ters. On several occasions, the mother awoke in the middle of the night to see three ghostly figures – nuns – standing at the foot of her bed.

The woman was, quite naturally, reluctant to frighten her daughter and so she kept the occurrences to herself. However, years later, the daughter revealed that she also had seen the spectral nuns in the house, but had also kept quiet so as not to alarm her mother.

The Blue Lady of Runnymede Road

Runnymede Road lies on the Red House Estate in Sunderland and one of the dwellings is reputed to be haunted by a ghost known as the 'Blue Lady'. Her epithet derives from the fact that she always appears to witnesses in a blue dress. Her general *modus operandi* is to float across the lounge towards the fireplace, where she then vanishes.

Many years ago, the local council were renovating the property and apparently found a pair of blue shoes in the chimney stack.

The Old Man of Ravenswood Road

A house in Ravenswood Road, which also lies within the boundaries of the aforementioned Red House Estate, is allegedly haunted by the ghost of an elderly gentleman. Tenants would retire to bed in the evening with everything seemingly normal. The following morning they would go downstairs

Runnymede Road, where a woman in a blue dress has been seen in a house in this street. Known as the 'Blue Lady', she is said to float across the lounge and disappear out of site when she reaches the fireplace.

to find that whilst they had slept the ghostly resident had moved various household objects. One former resident said that on one occasion she happened to look up the stairwell and could actually see the shade of the old man standing at the top.

The Ghostly Sea Dog of Villiers Street

Back in the early nineteenth century, a lodging house stood near the corner of High Street and Villiers Street. The rooms were almost exclusively taken by mariners, and as they were quite plush and beyond the financial reach of common seafarers, most of them were captains. It seems that on one occasion a ship docked at Sunderland and, after paying his crew, the captain made straight for the lodging house to rent a room. Unfortunately, it seems that one sailor had taken a grievance against the captain and decided that a face-to-face confrontation was the best way of sorting the matter out. This can sometimes be the case, but not after you have downed several pints of ale in a local tavern.

Enraged, the sailor made his way to the lodging house, entered, and brayed upon the door of the captain's room. As soon as the man opened the door, the sailor set upon him. The captain had no chance to defend himself and was beaten to death. To this day, those who enter that room say that it is icy cold even on the hottest of summer days. The ghost of the murdered man has

allegedly been seen at one of the windows, and – just for good measure – a secret passageway is said to lie underneath the building.

Hauntings on Nile Street

In July 1949, a family who lived in Nile Street reported that for the previous four weeks their lives had been made a misery by a ghost who had peered in through, and broken their windows, and generally made their lives hell on earth. The first inkling the family had that something was amiss came at 1.30 a.m., when they heard the back door of their house creaking, after which the interior lights were mysteriously switched on. The husband got up to investigate, but there was no one to be seen.

That was the first of many eerie incidents that culminated with no less than five windows being broken. Even stranger, the lady of the house discovered a brown paper parcel in her washhouse. When she opened it, she found it contained a ghoulish mask. Where it came from and who put it there has never been explained. Prior to these bizarre occurrences, an incident had taken place which some thought may have been connected with the alleged paranormal activity. The son of the couple had chanced upon two villains pinching lead from the roof of a nearby house and had confronted them. A chase ensued, but when the man caught up with the thieves one of them assaulted him

Nile Street – the scene of a haunting in June 1949, where for four weeks a family reported a whole host of frightening paranormal activity that eventually scared them from their home.

before they finally made good their escape. The only distinctive detail the man could give about his assailants was that they were 'well spoken'.

Naturally, many people were convinced that the men had returned to exact retribution on the man by smashing the windows and generally terrorising his family. Tempting though this theory is, in some respects it is unlikely. Within two days of the strange events starting, crowds had begun to gather and the police were paying regular visits to the dwelling. It seems highly unlikely that the two thieves would have continued their campaign of intimidation when there was such a chance of being seen and apprehended.

Another telling factor is that even if the two thieves had made it their business to attack the family home, this would not explain the many other incidents that occurred, such as the hearing of disembodied footsteps and the appearance of ghostly faces at the windows. To add insult to injury, the family started to receive letters from 'cranks', which only made their situation worse. Eventually they vacated the house and moved in with relatives.

Nile Street had already developed a reputation for fortean phenomena long before the above incident, however. In March 1909, a young miner was killed in a brawl with a number of youths from the East End who belonged to a notorious outfit known as the Nut Gang, and his ghost was said to walk Nile Street and surrounding alleyways. In later years, a Quaker burial ground was uncovered on the site, generating further gossip that the bizarre antics of previous years may have been of paranormal origin.

One of the most celebrated legends of Nile Street is centred around a building called Coronation Chambers, which stood on the corner of Nile Street and Coronation Street. Witnesses repeatedly testified that they had heard the sounds of footsteps and doors banging. On a number of occasions, a ghostly figure was seen strolling around the building, but whenever anyone tried to confront him he would simply disappear. One man was also violently tipped out of an easy chair by unseen hands.

A cleaner in a nearby pub had an unnerving experience when, early one morning, she saw a man standing in the bar even though the premises were still securely locked. Naturally, she asked the chap who he was and what he wanted, to which he replied, 'I'm looking for the foundry.' The cleaner grew suspicious and called the landlord into the bar, but when she turned around the man had disappeared. The premises were thoroughly searched and the doors were found to be perfectly secure. The mysterious interloper was never found and the consensus was that the cleaner had seen a ghost.

The Silver Street Tombstone

The East End of Sunderland used to contain some terrible slum dwellings before the First World War, but before then the same dwellings had been residences of distinction. To live there, one needed both prestige and money. As the dwelling houses aged, however, a number of them gained reputations of being haunted. Alan Tedder recalls the late Margaret Miller telling him of one such tale, of a ghost that allegedly haunted Silver Street in the early nineteenth century.

Number 9 Silver Street was at one time known as Lady Bowser House and when the grand owners departed for greener pastures, this fine old property became a tenement. Resident after resident told of how the curtains would be closed by unseen hands and that plates and other pieces of crockery on shelves would also rock back and forth.

On one occasion, a young chap was sitting alone in a room in Lady Bowser House whilst his parents and other family members were in an adjoining room. Suddenly, he screamed out, 'Oh, the man, the man!' What had actually happened to the young man must rate as one of the most incredible paranormal experiences of all time, if true of course. Whilst sitting in the chair, the apparition of a man seemed to stretch forth from the ceiling. Two firm hands grabbed the boy by the shoulders and proceeded to drag him upwards towards the ceiling. The entity then dropped him just as his parents came running into the room. The boy suffered a broken shoulder from the incident.

Later, another family moved into the same premises. So shocked were they by the ghosts that manifested that they fled, leaving behind all their worldly possessions. As they stood outside, they watched in horrible fascination as everything they owned was thrown out of the windows onto the ground below. Rumours began to circulate that a 'terrible murder' had once been committed there and that one of the ghosts was actually the restless spirit of the victim. Other tales suggest that a man had committed suicide after a romantic relationship ended.

In 1900, extensive work was carried out on the building and part of it was demolished. Workmen discovered a tombstone sticking out of the ground, which was obviously of great age. They carefully removed it and brushed off the dirt, only to find that the words engraved upon it had almost completely worn away. However, they could just make out the numerals 2 and 3. Whether this tombstone was connected to the haunting in any way, I cannot say.

The Secret Vault

Also in Silver Street stood Pemberton Hall, which was allegedly haunted by a 'stately old lady' who wore a long, trailing silk gown. On every sighting, she was seen walking either up or down the stairwell.

In later years, when the house was demolished, an elaborately constructed vault was found which ran all the way from the hall to Burleigh Street and then down to the quayside. The origins of the vault are uncertain and it was filled with a noxious, musty odour. The consensus is that it had been used – and possibly even built – by local smugglers.

The Burleigh Street Nun

In 1942, a resident in a lodging house in Burleigh Street had been 'out on the pop' one evening and, having imbibed a surfeit of alcohol, found it rather difficult to negotiate the stairs that

An artist's impression of the Burleigh Street nun that was seen in 1942. (Courtesy of Julie Olley)

led to his apartment. Tired, he simply slumped down onto the stairs and fell asleep. At some point, he was awoken by a peculiar swishing noise, similar the sound a dress makes as it glides across a wooden floor. He opened his eyes and was astonished to see the image of a nun standing in front of him, surrounded by an intense white light.

The Moorgate Street Washerwoman

In 1933, a Mrs Close lived in Moorgate Street – quite happily, by all accounts. Late one evening, she happened to be chatting in the street with some neighbours when one of them

An artist's impression of the Moorgate Street washerwoman that was seen by a number of people back in 1933. (Courtesy of Julie Olley)

drew attention to something rather strange. Floating down the street towards them was the apparition of an old woman with a wicker basket in her hand. Terrified, they all ran into the nearest dwelling and dived into the same bed as the householder's sleeping husband. On listening to the women's tale, he calmly told them he too had seen it – the ghost of a woman who had been murdered in a local washhouse. She had repeatedly been seen walking the length of the street at night before vanishing.

Peg Leg of Zion Street

At the end of the nineteenth century, a tenement block in Zion Street in Sunderland was apparently plagued by the shade of a man with a wooden leg. Residents in Zion Street often heard the distinctive sound of the one-legged man making his way up the stairs. Eventually they named him 'Peg Leg', which, although perfectly apt, was somewhat unimaginative.

The Hazy Ghosts of Spout Lane

A woman and her spouse were walking down Spout Lane one evening when the man was caught out by an urgent call of nature. He went to relieve himself by a nearby tree and left his wife standing at the roadside, but she decided to walk on ahead.

Spout Lane in Washington Village; it was here where two 'hazy' ghostly figures were once seen late at night, and on more than one occasion.

After a short while, she became concerned as her husband had not caught up with her and she retraced her steps back. A little further down the lane she could see 'two hazy figures' moving about on the path. The woman made her way over to where her husband was standing and pointed out the strangers. He too could see them and, like his wife, was astonished. Eventually they disappeared and the couple made their way home as fast as possible.

Later, the woman happened to mention the incident to a friend and was amazed to hear that she had seen the spectral figures also whilst walking her dog down the lane one evening. It later transpired that a man – also walking his dog – had seen the same two entities acting bizarrely near Dame Dorothy Hall.

4

PEOPLE, OBJECTS AND MISCELLANEOUS PLACES

The Cauld Lad of Hylton

The legend of the Cauld Lad of Hylton is one of the most famous supernatural stories in the north east of England. Hylton Castle was built in AD 1072, and was once the baronial seat of a powerful and wealthy family. At some point during its subsequent history, usually believed to be the opening decade of the seventeenth century, a murder took place at the castle and since then persistent rumours have circulated indicating that the ruin is haunted. A host of variations to the story exist, and separating fact from fiction is now almost impossible. Nevertheless, there are certain core elements to the story that are always present.

The Lord of the Castle in 1609 was Robert Hylton, who has been described rather incongruously, as we shall see, as a 'gentleman'. At some time, there was a stable hand named Roger Skelton employed at the Castle. Roger was, by all accounts, an ami- able youngster who, although not well educated, always had a smile upon his face and a friendly greeting for everyone who passed him by. The baron and master of the castle was not so well disposed to those around him, and was known to fly into an apoplectic rage at the least provocation. One day, apparently, young Roger fell asleep whilst he was supposed to be working. It seems the Lord had a journey to go on and had instructed that his horse be prepared. Skelton had not prepared the horse prior to falling asleep and it was not ready for his master's departure. The Lord could not let such a gross misdemeanour go unpunished, of course, and apparently had no alternative but to run the sleeping youngster through repeatedly with a pitchfork. No doubt he slept well that night, knowing that he had served justice well and rid the land of such a menace as young Roger. No wonder the people of Sunderland (allegedly) hated his guts.

An old photograph of Hylton Castle, haunted by the 'Cauld Lad', and taken around 1880 by a Mrs D. Moon. (Courtesy of Newcastle Libraries and Information Service)

An old line drawing depicting Hylton Castle back in 1800. (Courtesy of Newcastle Libraries and Information Service)

There was considerable disquiet in the district, and it was alleged – correctly – that Hylton had murdered Roger. There was, of course, no realistic proposition of a wealthy and influential man like Hylton ever being prosecuted for the murder of a mere stable boy. A 'witness' was found who testified that the Lord had accidentally struck Roger with a scythe on his thigh whilst mowing. The notion that the Lord of the Castle would engage in farming labour was patently ridiculous, of course, but it was all that the Coroner needed to dilute the accusation and, later in the year, Bishop William Jameson pardoned the Lord for Roger's manslaughter.

Shortly after the murder, to avoid answering any embarrassing questions, Hylton had the lad's body dumped in a nearby lake. (The lake has since been drained in more recent times and the skeleton of a young boy was indeed found at the bottom.) Shortly thereafter, the ghost of Roger made his first appearance at Hylton Castle.

At the same time that Roger's ghost started to appear at Hylton Castle, other supernatural phenomena, which carried all the hallmarks of poltergeist activity, began to manifest themselves. One evening, the servants awoke to the sound of horrendous crashing noises coming from the banqueting hall. On arrival, they were stunned to see the Lord's best pewter ware being thrown by invisible hands across the room. By the time the polt-like activity had finished, the hall looked as if a herd of cows had careered through it at full pelt.

So frequently did this display of activity manifest itself, that the staff eventually decided not to bother cleaning up the banqueting hall at night, and instead left it until the following morning. To their astonishment, however, as soon as they decided upon this course of action the ghost had a change of heart. On entering the banqueting hall the next day, they found that it had been cleaned and tidied to a degree that would have made the most fastidious homemaker proud!

And thus the pattern was established. When the hall was left tidy, the poltergeist would wreak havoc and mayhem as soon as the lights were out. Should the servants leave it in a state of disorder, he would have it gleaming like a new pin by dawn. The staff soon learned how to play the game, and took bizarre satisfaction in having seemingly trained the poltergeist to do their work for them. Eventually, the Lord and his entourage tired of the presence and apparently worked out a cunning plan by which they would trick him into 'departing to the better place'. Before the operation could be enacted, however, the poltergeist seems to have gotten wind of their cunning. That night, the staff allegedly heard it utter a chilling stanza:

Wae's me, Wae's me.
The acorn is not yet
Fallen from the tree
That's to grow the wood,
That's to make the cradle,

That's to rock the bairn,

That's to grow a man,

That's to lay me!

They tried, nevertheless. Relying on an old superstition, the servants believed that if they could trick the entity into donning a green cloak and hood, he would be forced to leave them alone. The next evening the correct garment was left out, draped over a chair, and the lights dimmed. The staff, or at least those who were brave enough, hid in darkened corners and watched.

At midnight, the spectre appeared and duly donned the green cloak. He then proceeded to dance, skip and cavort around the banqueting hall, before finally exclaiming, 'Here's a cloak! Here's a hood. The cauld lad o' Hylton will do no mair good!'

One tradition has it that the ghost of Roger was headless, which would certainly fit in with some appearances of the ghost who was also said to appear without a head at times. It may be, then, that the ghost and the poltergeist were one and the same, and that the former was simply an incarnation of the latter. Some have suggested that the word 'cauld' (a Wearside colloquialism for 'cold') should really be 'cowed' – an old term that actually means 'headless'.

To this day, the ghost of Roger is still occasionally glimpsed on the battlements of Hylton Castle. Sunderland researcher Alan Tedder has reputedly documented several sightings, including one of a local miner who saw 'the Lad' as he walked home from his shift at the pit. He was severely traumatised by the incident and was never quite the same afterwards.

In 1912, a chap called John Straw lived in Castletown. John recalled that late one night he had been drinking at the Three Horse Shoes Inn at Usworth, and upon leaving at closing time he was cycling past the castle when a thought struck him. Due to having drunk too much it probably seemed like a good idea at the time, but as things turned out it was anything but. Incredibly, John shouted out a challenge to the Cauld Lad, warning him exactly what he would do if he got his hands on him. John was stunned when a voice came from the vicinity of the castle stating that it accepted his challenge. Now, if disrespecting the Cauld Lad was stupid, what John did next bordered on lunacy. He actually dismounted from his bike and staggered around in the dark looking for the Cauld Lad so he could engage in fisticuffs with him. Well, you have to admire his guts.

At some point, he stumbled into the muddy beck nearby and there before him was a terrible sight indeed. It was not the Cauld Lad of Hylton. Worse, it was PC 27 Kitchen from Castletown Police Office, who had been mimicking the ghost for a laugh at Straw's expense. Twelve years went by and, in 1924, Straw happened to be cycling past the castle with two workmates when he spotted a lonely figure sitting on a wall. As his pals seemed not to have spotted the chap, he decided to have a laugh at their

The remains of Hylton Castle today, taken by the author using infra-red film.

expense. You would have thought he had learnt his lesson the first time, but never mind.

'Hey, lads, look!' he shouted, 'Is that the Cauld Lad sitting there?'

'Aye!' boomed forth a voice from where the stranger was sitting. Straw and his two pals, perhaps sensing that this was not PC 27 Kitchen, pedalled home as fast as they could.

To my knowledge, Straw did not chance his arm with the Cauld Lad for a third time.

In 1950, a watchman at the Castle claimed that the Lad had put out all his warning lamps, as well as his brazier.

In 1885, there was an establishment called Park House Farm at Hylton Castle. A Mrs Graham, who later ended up marrying the farmer, confirmed the legend of the Cauld Lad. She had actu-ally worked at the castle in that year, when the resident was a Lieutenant Colonel James Charles Briggs. Mrs Graham recalled that once, whilst working alone in a corridor which was locked at either end, she suddenly felt 'an unseen body' rush past her. On another occasion, she also heard a coach and horses pull up before the main door of the castle. The following morning she asked fellow staff who had arrived the previous night, and was taken aback to learn that nobody had called at the castle at all. Unnerved, she resigned her position. Actually, the spectral coach of Hylton Castle is a lesser-known aspect of the Cauld Lad tale. Anthony Ettrick – who died in 1883 and whose influential family had lived in the vicinity for years – often spoke of the ghostly coach that would race up the front drive of his home at North Hylton.

The Cauld Lad was also said to have appeared in a local pub. A bookmaker from Washington was drinking there one day, in 1966, when he was suddenly confronted by 'a white-faced spectre dressed in black'. The man was actually related to the family who ran the pub back then and recounted how, one night after closing time, he, his wife and their relatives were sitting in the lounge, which was illuminated by the lights from behind the bar. The bookmaker noticed that his wife suddenly 'gave a startled look'. He followed her gaze and saw the same eerie figure standing behind the others that were present. He rubbed his eyes and looked again, only to find the spectre had vanished. It was claimed that the Cauld Lad had appeared several times in the pub over the previous three years.

In 1942, a chap from Hall Gardens, West Boldon, had been drinking in the Black Horse Pub with two friends one night when they decided to put the legend of the Cauld Lad to the test. They hit upon the idea of holding a 'vigil' there overnight, so at closing time they headed off over the fields and upon reaching the castle at 11.20 pm., they surreptitiously gained entry through a window on the second floor. Once inside they struck a match, lit a candle and started to play a game of cards.

Midnight came and suddenly the three men heard a terrible din from the floor above. They were so shocked that they all jumped to their feet and knocked over the candle in the process. Then, to their horror, they heard the sound of footsteps. Worse, the spectral footfalls seemed to be drawing closer to their room. As they listened in horrible fascination, the footsteps seemed to pass by their room and head for the kitchen area below. Without further ado, they fled, and who can blame them?

In July 1981, police investigated a complaint that a number of young men were discharging air rifles from the battlements of the castle. Two officers were dispatched and whilst in the castle grounds both heard an eerie sound 'like heavy breathing' that 'seemed to arise out of the bowels of the earth'. Thinking that someone might be trapped, the castle custodian was called in as well as the fire brigade. They raised the turntable ladder up to the battlements and a fruitless search, lasting an hour, took place. No one was found on the premises.

Wearside William?

I never knew this, but it has been alleged that the infamous bodysnatcher and murderer, William Burke (of the Burke and Hare infamy) learned, or at least began, his gruesome grave-robbing trade right here in Wearside, while he was working on the new pier in Sunderland's south dock with his fellow Irish friend and partner in crime, William Hare. Burke and Hare were skilled labourers that came from Ireland in the early 1800s, and it is thought that during their time in Wearside they hatched their appalling plan of raiding graveyards and digging up the newly deceased so they could sell them for the easy money. Doctors would use the bodies for medical research and, by all accounts, paid quite handsomely for them.

Legend has it that Holy Trinity Churchyard in Sunderland was where Burke would dig up fresh corpses and deliver them to local doctors so they could carry out their explorative research. Eventually, rumour has it, things began to go wrong for Burke after a young man that he had been working with slipped and fell, subsequently breaking his neck. The young man was said to have had no relatives or friends in the region, therefore his body was put away in storage until the authorities could bury him. The burial, as we shall see, never happened. Not long after the body was placed into storage, it mysteriously disappeared without a trace. However, the day after the body went missing it was reported that employee Burke had been observed by a witness making his way through the yards and heading off towards Sunderland town centre pushing a wooden cart that looked to be rather heavy. When questioned, it is alleged that he told his employers that he borrowed the cart because he needed to move some heavy belongings, after which he promptly returned to work. Given what we now know about the horrendous crimes of Messrs Burke and Hare, it is not hard to imagine what Burke was really doing that night. (I keep using the word 'alleged' as I feel this tale must be taken with a pinch of salt.)

It was, and still is, presumed to this day that Burke would have most

The Piers at Wearside said to be the haunt of notorious bodysnatchers Burke and Hare before they travelled north to Edinburgh.

The Shipping Staithes (also known as 'the Drops') in Sunderland around the time that William Burke was alleged to have worked there. (Courtesy of Newcastle Libraries and Information Service)

certainly known that if the body was to disappear then pretty much nothing could have been done about it. Therefore, it is surmised that he decided there and then to take the body and offer it to doctors for medical dissection – just another lifeless corpse in the eyes of Burke with the added bonus of a few extra quid in his pocket. This, as legend suggests, is what was thought to have occurred. The tale goes that he found a doctor in the Hendon area of Sunderland and successfully delivered the deceased young man to him. If this is true, and bear in mind that we have no way of knowing for sure, then this could well be one of the very first instances of bodysnatching by William Burke. Legend also suggests that because he was observed acting in a strange manner, and subsequently questioned because of it, he became a little nervous, as you would expect, and decided to up sticks and move to Edinburgh. Not wanting to make the journey alone, he travelled with his old companion and fellow Irishman, William Hare.

Upon their arrival at Edinburgh, they continued with their grave robbing and it was in Edinburgh that they stayed. Not long after arriving, they hooked up with Dr Knox who, of course, was all too happy to purchase their corpses. After a while, when the grave robbing became all too well-known to the authorities, guards and lookouts were assigned to all the cemeteries in an effort to quell their odious crimes. But this did not stop Burke and Hare; they wanted to keep their steady income so they decided that rather than dig the bodies fresh out the ground, they simply had to begin killing people themselves – at least now there was no digging to be done in the dead of night.

This began the appalling and gruesome chain of murders in the Edinburgh region and in total over sixteen innocent people fell victim to the evil of Burke and Hare. Eventually they were caught and Burke was publicly hanged in front of 25,000 people on 28 January 1828. William Hare was offered a pardon if he confessed to the murders that he took part in and it was this confession that led to Burke being hanged. Hare was set free and it is believed he was last spotted in Carlisle in 1868. It is interesting to note that a mask was made of William Burke's face before and after his hanging. These are called death masks and it was common practice in those days to have them made for such notable individuals. I have been fortunate enough to see both of these historic artefacts and examine them for myself and what a privilege that was. To hold William Burke's death mask moulded from his actual face was an incredible but eerie experience, not many people get that chance. The William Burke death masks are now held at the Museum of the Royal College of Surgeons in Edinburgh. Burke's skeletal remains are held just a stone's throw away in the anatomy collection at Edinburgh University. How ironic would it be if his remains were stolen?

In regards to the alleged ghost of William Burke, we must journey back to Wearside if we are to take the account as true. It is said that William Burke once worked on the banks of the River Wear, which is now a ship-yard and steel works, and according to radio presenter for the North East and celebrity ghost hunter, Alan Robson, many people have claimed it was haunted. In his most interesting book, *Ghostly Trails and Grisly Trails* (Virgin, 1992) he tells the aforementioned story of Burke and Hare, along with the har-rowing ghost story that features an ugly looking, broad-shouldered individual that seemed to have had arms some-what longer than they should have been. Apparently, this spectral form has been seen walking around on the site at the shipyard, and has been seen mooch-ing about on the cranes and other 'steel structures'. The most disturb-ing tale of this Wearside spook comes from a local man called Mr Phillips. Robson explains that Mr Phillips was

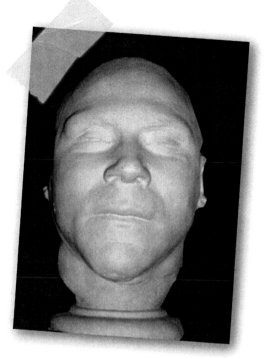

William Burke's facial cast, taken shortly before his execution. (Author's collection)

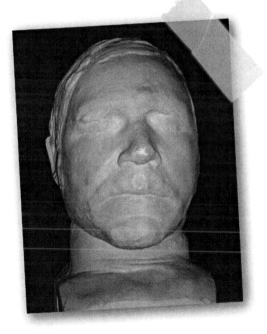

William Burke's death mask after his execution. Note the swelling of his facial features. Both masks are held at the Museum of the Royal College of Surgeons in Edinburgh. (Author's collection)

working the nightshift one night and was sitting alone having his break at about eleven o'clock when suddenly he heard a commotion coming from the outside toilet. Venturing outside to see what was going on, he noticed his three workers on the other side of the yard working away, as they should have been. Since no one else was supposed to be on site, he now wondered just who had made the noise that was seemingly coming from the toilets. Robson goes on to say that Mr Phillips pulled open the toilet door, half expecting to catch an intruder, and was surprised to see what he described as a 'ape like man' crouching over. He [the ape-man] looked up and then charged towards Mr Phillips, who tried to apprehend the strange prowler and swung a punch at him. The punch failed to make contact with anything. From the momentum, he spun around and fell to the ground banging his head on the loo seat. Robson finishes off with a quote from Mr Phillips, who Robson interviewed not long after the event took place, and says, 'There was no way he could get past me unless he went *through* me. I am certain he did.'

Fascinating tale to say the least, but I will close this section with two final thoughts on the whole legend. The first is this that I have no doubt that Mr Phillips was telling the truth about his encounter and I am quite prepared to believe paranormal incidences have occurred down in the old shipyards and steel works. However, there is nothing at all in this tale to suggest the phantom that haunts this area is really the mass-murdering, grave-robbing criminal William Burke. He may have worked here in times gone by, and maybe he did begin his grave robbing activities in Wearside as legends suggest – although some Burke and Hare historians will no doubt beg to differ – but to link William Burke to the shipyard phantom to me is a rather unwise decision as all the evidence is entirely circumstantial.

The second point is that there is, however, one piece of evidence that does interest me somewhat and it is that it is stated in the above text that Mr Phillips was confronted with an 'ugly looking, broad-shouldered individual that seems to have arms somewhat longer than they should be'. Having looked closely at the skeletal remains of William Burke it is clear to see that he is indeed a broad-shouldered man, furthermore, his arms are incredibly long and when standing in an upright position his hands are almost hanging down by his knees! This seems to fit perfectly with the testimonies of those that have seen the ghost in the old ship-yard and steel works, including that of Mr Phillips. This is still circumstantial evidence, but as I am sure the reader will agree, it is a very compelling, or should I say, uncanny coincidence, but perhaps that is all it is? It would indeed be an eerie, yet enchanting thought, however, to have one of the world's most notorious serial killers/bodys-natchers residing here in the north east of England in spectral from – I always keep an open mind.

Sunderland Empire Theatre

The Sunderland Empire Theatre stands on High Street West in the centre of Sunderland, and is reportedly haunted by a number of ghosts. One, believe it or not, is thought by some to be that of comic legend and 'Carry On' star, Sid James (1913–1976). Sid James did indeed perform there on many occasions and, unfortunately for him, he died on stage there too. On 26 April 1976, Sid walked onto the stage for the last time and suffered a fatal heart attack in front of the 2,000-strong audience, who all thought it was part of the act. He was starring in *The Mating Game* with his co-star Audrey Jeans on its opening night when he collapsed. It was a sad and tragic end to one of the world's funniest movie stars.

The Empire Theatre in Sunderland City Centre. Carry On star Sid James died on stage here in 1976 and his ghost is said to haunt the premises to this day.

It is said that not long after his death, people visiting the theatre began to get an eerie sense of his presence, especially actors and actresses that just happened to be using his old dressing room. I have learned recently that one or two big stars that have appeared there have indeed claimed to see the ghost of Sid himself in the theatre; although, none of them will openly admit to it, much to the relief of the theatre's management. Fellow comedian Les Dawson (1931–1993) was, however, one of the famous stars that claimed to have experienced something very strange while attending the Empire Theatre in 1992, but never told anyone exactly what it was he saw. He never returned to appear there again after revealing 'What I saw was the worst experience of my life'. Some say it could have been Sid's ghost, but I guess we will never know for sure, as he took his secret to the grave.

More recently, in 2006, Mike Hallowell was invited to the theatre to cover the thirtieth anniversary of Sid James' death for his 'WraithScape' column. A three-part feature was written up, telling the history, the alleged ghosts of the Empire, and, of course, the death of Sid James. During his visit to the theatre, he was shown all around the premises by one of the staff while conducting his interviews. He had his EVP (Electronic Voice Phenomena) machine with him and while explaining to the staff just what EVPs were, he made a recording that astonished both the member of staff he was with, and himself.

Mike takes up the story:

Joanne Wilkins was the Press & Marketing Co-ordinator at the Sunderland Empire at the time, and invited me up to this grand old theatre to discuss the 30th anniversary of Sid's death. Rumours that the ghost of Sid James still haunted the Empire had appeared regularly in the press, but I wanted to see the place for myself, see if I could maybe 'pick up' anything paranormal as I wandered from room to room and gallery to gallery.

Our first stop was a rather gloomy basement filled with props. A stack of old chairs that looked very '70s', two tailors' dummies, a music system, cardboard boxes, sheet music … a veritable treasure trove of memories, each one clinging to a play that had enthralled the region's public at some time in the past. Oh, how I'd love to have had a good old rummage. Alas, there wasn't anything paranormal to be seen or heard. If Sid James was watching us he certainly wasn't making his presence felt. I gazed around the basement just before we left and even took some photographs, hoping against hope that I'd immortalise on celluloid a passing spirit or two. But no, it was not to be.

Melvyn James, the theatre manager, had confessed to me when I interviewed him that there was one place in the theatre that did make him feel a little uneasy; the upper gallery which had only recently been opened up again to the public. Intriguingly, Joanne told me that she too felt a bit

'spooked' up there and preferred not to go up to the gallery without the lights on. Neither Joanne or Melvyn could definitely state that the place was haunted and, much as I'd have liked them to, I appreciated their candour and refusal to milk the media cow by 'talking up' a ghost that perhaps didn't exist.

Whilst Joanne and I sat quietly in the gallery I made some digital sound recordings, hoping to pick up some of the mysterious EVP (Electronic Voice Phenomena) that researchers love to capture and analyse. We played the recording back, and again there seemed to be nothing; not even the briefest of dirty cackles from the greatest Carry On star of all. Later I downloaded the audio recording into my computer and boosted the volume. When I'd listened to it with Joanne we'd heard nothing unusual, but with the volume turned up something very strange became evident. Towards the end of the recording you can clearly hear me say to Joanne, 'The strange thing is that sometimes you can record things and you don't hear anything at the time, but then when I go home and put it on my computer and play it back you can hear things … voices …'

At this point in the recording a woman's voice − not Joanne's − can be clearly heard saying, 'We'll have to tell them …' followed by another woman's voice laughing cheekily. The really weird thing was that the voices occurred at the very spot on the tape where I can be heard explaining to

The stage at the Sunderland Empire where Sid James took his last breath. (Courtesy of Newcastle Libraries and Information Service)

Joanne how some anomalous sounds can only be heard later when the recording is downloaded onto a computer – the very thing I'd just done.

Fascinating to say the very least, but whether Sid James haunts the Empire Theatre or not we just don't know for sure, however, phantasms of a much older vintage are rumoured to be present. Long before Sid's sad demise, other mysteries had already entrenched themselves in the theatre's history. The greatest of these enigmas is the strange disappearance of Molly Moselle. It is said that on the afternoon of Friday, 14 January 1949, Molly, who was stage manager for the Ivor Novello play *The Dancing Years*, left the theatre to post some letters. Others claim she went to her lodgings first and then on to purchase a birthday card for the actor Barry Sinclair, who later appeared in *It Ain't Half Hot Mum* with Windsor Davies. In any event, Molly did not return and just what happened to her is still a mystery.

It is thought that the last person to see Molly alive was an Empire employee who lived in an upstairs flat nearby. He happened to look out of a window and saw Molly walking down the road. Could the employee have been mistaken? It is unlikely, because Molly was always a flamboyant dresser and had been wearing bright orange slacks and a matching top. The employee watched as Molly slipped into the narrow alley between Garden Place and Eden Street presumably for her premature appointment with destiny.

Many rumours have circulated about Molly's fate. Some claim that she was seen drinking with a 'mysterious Russian sailor' in a pub called the Brougham Arms. Others say it wasn't the Brougham Arms at all, but the nearby Dun Cow and that she was in the company of not one sailor, but several. Personally, I don't think the Empire employee was the last person to see Molly alive, as I suspect she was murdered. Did she meet a belligerent drunkard in that alley? Did he waylay Molly and then kill her? No one can be sure, but the rumours that she committed suicide due to her convoluted love life just don't make sense.

Of course, we cannot be sure that Molly is actually dead. Even back then, there were sightings of her at railway stations, pubs and shops. She was even reputed to have put in an appearance back at the theatre before disappearing again. In 1960, a badly decomposed body, which roughly fitted Molly's size, was dragged out of the River Wear. In the absence of DNA testing, however, no one could conclusively say that it was the corpse of Miss Moselle and the truth is the odds are greatly against it.

Soon, rumours were circulating that the ghost of Molly Moselle was haunting the theatre, particularly the bar upstairs. None of the staff currently employed there seem to have seen anything, although there is talk of a 'Grey Lady' being seen both in the aforementioned bar and on a nearby stairwell. Is the Grey Lady Molly Moselle? If there really is a Grey Lady, she may well be the spectre of someone who died long before poor Molly even went missing. There are just so many unanswered questions.

The Phantom in the Infirmary

Chester Road was in existence from 1823 to 1867, and was once the site of an old hospital, which was known to Wearsiders as the Royal Infirmary. The Royal Infirmary was founded in 1794 and since then it has relocated on a number of occasions. The last Royal Infirmary was situated on New Durham Road and had been there since 1867; it is now used as flats. Currently, Sunderland's main hospital is called the Sunderland Royal Hospital and is located on Kayll road, which is spookily close to the old Chester Road hospital site. Not a lot of people know this, but the old Chester Road infirmary was subjected to a haunting. In fact, it was haunted by a number of shades and spectres, and there have been many harrowing accounts told by the staff and its patients of spirits

Sunderland's Royal Infirmary. (Courtesy of Newcastle Libraries and Information Service)

'coming in' from time to time. One of its former resident ghosts, sadly, was in fact one of its former patients who had spent some time in the hospital as she neared the end of her long life. Eventually, after much deteriorating, she passed away.

By all accounts, however, this was not the last the infirmary saw of her, not by a long chalk. For whatever reason, this particular individual decided that she was 'staying put' at the Royal Infirmary, putting in her ethereal appearances every now and again after her death. Not a lot is known about the ghosts – or the former ghosts – of the old hospital, which is quite sad as tales such as these deserve to be fully researched and remembered. What *is* known about the shade of the Royal Infirmary is that all she wore was a nightdress – presumably the one she wore during her time at the hospital – and when she was seen, she was seen only from the mid-section up! It was as though her ghost was walking around on a floor situated on a lower level than the one the bewildered onlooker was on – as if the present floor had been raised.

There are many stories detailing ghost sightings just like this one, such as the ghostly dwarf-like figure of Woodchester Mansion, who is seen darting around the basement area of the building. It has been suggested that the original level of the floor was lower than what it is now, thus making the spectre seem shorter than he actually is. Of course, we have the world famous sighting, in 1953, of the phantom army of Roman soldiers that marched their way through the cellars of Treasurer's House in York – apparently on their knees. Of course, it transpired that they were really walking on the original Roman road (*Via Decumana*), which lay approximately 12 inches below the cellar floor.

The Fulwell Phantoms

According to local researcher, Mike Hallowell the Fulwell area of Sunderland was 'gripped by ghost fever back in September of 1932'. It appears that a misty phantom was observed drifting across a nearby playing field that was being used by the locals as a football pitch. The observer, an individual going by the name of Joe Porter, was strolling along one day on his way past the field that stood by the old Fulwell School, when he encountered the denizen from beyond. Adamant that he had seen an actual ghost, he began to tell his tale of the misty apparition to his friends and family, and the story soon spread around the area like wildfire.

Back in those days, when people heard about an alleged spectral sighting, it would not be a surprise to see masses of excited and, more often than not, obsessed, individuals flocking near to the spot of 'ghost sighting', in order to see this inhabitant of the Otherworld for themselves. In this instance, it was no different.

Of course, it was only to be expected that a number of folk would 'claim' to see the apparition. Over the next week or so, a number of reports came in of a similar sort of ghostly apparition, but, oddly, they were not reported in the same area where Joe had seen it. Sightings allegedly occurred in the local cemetery (no surprise there then) and in some nearby allotment gardens. When the ghost reached a main road, however, according to Mike, it would disappear into thin air. One wonders why this would occur.

Mike also told me that a retired schoolteacher and local resident of Fulwell 'often' saw a precession of spectral monks as she was walking her dogs. The monks were seen on a stretch of track that was once used by real monks as they made their way to nearby St Peter's Church – although Mike does articulate, 'Whether this was true or not I cannot say'. He then told me, 'To my knowledge the ghost monks of Fulwell have not been seen in recent times.'

One wonders why the Fulwell phantoms have not been observed recently. Perhaps they are similar to most stereotypical ghosts and are only seen every 100 years or so? Perhaps they have materialised but no one was there to see them? Another reason could be that they were observed during a recent appearance, but the witness or witnesses decided to keep quiet about it for fear of ridicule and scorn. One other possibility remains, of course, that there has been no ghost sightings recently simply because the area has

An artist's representation of a precession of phantom monks that have been seen in the Fulwell area of Sunderland (Courtesy of Julie Olley)

never been haunted! I think the latter is unlikely, although admittedly this is not a 'proof positive' case. It would be interesting to find out more regarding these wonderful tales of apparitions, and I would of course welcome any feedback from locals who might just know a little more detail regarding them. Who knows, someone reading these very words might have actually seen the ghosts that reside in Fulwell.

The Haunted Laundry of Toward Road

In 1891, there stood an old steam laundry in Toward Road, Sunderland. For those who could afford it, it was an ideal way to avoid having to 'poss' a basketful of smalls every Friday. Without the benefit of a modern washing machine, doing the laundry could be backbreaking business. At the steam laundry, therefore, business was brisk. In fact, it was so brisk that the owners had been forced to build an extension onto the rear of the premises to enlarge the number of washers and presses.

The time was precisely 8 p.m. on Monday, 7 September. There were three young girls and an equal number of men in the washroom – housed in the older part of the building. Other workers were scattered throughout the building, including the new extension. The girls each worked at their own bench; two at one end of the room, and one at the other. The girl who was working on her own had her bench near two doors, which led to two smaller rooms one of which was used for storage and the other was the supervisor's office. Without warning, the girl suddenly asked the supervisor if he would have any objection to her moving her bench closer to those of the other two girls. The supervisor – obviously not over-endowed with the milk of human kindness – told her to stop being so picky and to get on with her work.

'I have to go downstairs for some more soap – I'll be back in a minute, so no slacking,' he added. The supervisor had hardly descended to the next landing when he heard a bloodcurdling scream emanate from the washroom that he had just left. Fearing someone had suffered a dreadful accident, he raced back up the stairs as fast as his legs could carry him. Actually, he was fortunate not to be knocked over as two of the girls raced down the stairwell in a state of extreme excitement.

'There's a ghost up there!' screamed one of the young girls, hardly stopping to draw breath. Now the supervisor, despite his cantankerous nature, seems to have been made of sterner stuff. Ghost or no ghost, he would not be kept out of his own washroom. As he entered, he was horrified to see the third girl – the one who had wanted to move her bench – lying prostrate on the floor. Fortunately, she had only fainted. He gently sat her up and revived her.

'What happened?'

'We saw a ghost, that's what happened! That's why I wanted to move my bench closer to the other two, because I could see it in the storage room walking around!'

The other two girls backed up her story. All three were adamant that they had seen the same, ethereal figure walk from the storage room to the supervisor's office on several occasions. Curiously, it never returned the way it had come.

The girl who had wanted to move her workbench had requested to do so because, on one occasion, it had actually walked within 4ft of her and she felt that this was distinctly too close for comfort. I am unsure what happened to the Tower Road laundry ghost. The sands of time have gently washed away the conclusion to this strange tale, although the spook may still inhabit the building to this very day.

Phantom Footfalls at the New Arcade

Joe Parkin was the caretaker of the New Arcade in High Street West, a busy retail establishment. The arcade ran from High Street to St Thomas Street, and visitors were always given a warm welcome by Joe and his beloved dog that seemed to be employed as a canine security guard or watchdog.

The arcade was demolished in the early 1970s, but not before it had written itself into Wearside's haunted history. The first recorded incident of paranormal activity occurred in September 1966, when employees at the arcade claimed that they could hear the sound of feet walking across the floor of the storeroom above their heads. Some suggested that the noises may have been 'echoing' from an adjoining property, but subsequent investigations apparently ruled this out. Mystified by the eerie footsteps, the shop assistants set a trap to catch the elusive intruder and stretched cords across the storeroom floor, then listened intently from downstairs. Once again the bizarre footfalls could be heard and then – a bang and a crash!

Convinced that their trap had worked and that the intruder had tripped over the cords, the shopkeepers dashed upstairs. To their amazement, they found that the room was empty. Disturbingly, though, they also noticed that the storeroom was as cold as ice. From this point on, the ghost seemed to spend less time pacing around the storeroom and ventured into the arcade shops. Sales assistants noticed that lights would mysteriously turn themselves on and off, and on one occasion, a manager found a fifteen-year-old employee rooted to the floor with fear. Joe Parkin was apparently sceptical of the stories at first, but soon changed his mind after he awoke in his bed to find a ghostly hand stroking his face, followed by the sound of retreating footsteps. His faithful hound thereafter refused to enter the haunted storeroom.

Today, a telephone exchange stands on the site of the old arcade and the spectral footfalls have fallen silent.

John Wesley and Mrs Hobson

John Wesley is well known for being one of the progenitors of the Methodist Movement, but what is often overlooked about this great religious thinker is his unshakeable belief in the concept of communication between the living and the dead. Today, many Christians eschew a belief in spiritualism and some even believe that it is a demonic practice encouraged by the Devil himself. Wesley, though, had no such misgivings. He often wrote about his thoughts on the matter and more than once commented on the abilities of the acclaimed Sunderland medium Elizabeth Hobson.

Elizabeth experienced strange 'visitations' from childhood. She regularly claimed to hear 'angelic music',

John Wesley, the founder of the Methodist movement, and a supporter of Sunderland medium Mrs Hobson. (Wikipedia)

the source of which could never be rationally explained. In later years, she was contacted by the spirits of those who had passed on, many of them sailors who had tragically drowned at sea. Such experiences were, of course, sad. Death, although an integral part of the human condition, is nevertheless unpleasant, particularly for those left behind to grieve for the loss of a loved one. Still, even today, a growing number of people take comfort from the fact that the dead can return to this earthly plane and reassure their friends and relatives that they are still 'living', albeit in the spirit world.

Elizabeth never denied the reality of her visions and her sincerity captivated the attention of Wesley strongly.

As her competence as a medium grew, Elizabeth started to receive visitations from the spirit of a deceased old man who, it seems, had not been a particularly nice person before his demise. He had been cruel, callous and short-tempered. Yet, he chose to visit Hobson and discuss all manner of legal affairs with her, including the disposal of property. Perhaps his spirit was wracked with guilt about his previous behaviour, who knows?

In May 1768, Elizabeth began to experience a different kind of vision. Whereas she had previously predominantly been contacted by the dead, she then also started to see apparitions of the living. In every case, the person she saw died shortly afterwards. They would appear to Elizabeth surrounded in a glowing light, or 'luminosity', imminently before their passing.

Charles Wesley, John's brother, was somewhat more sceptical about Elizabeth's claims, but John had few, if any, doubts, particularly when she said that she had been visited by the spirit of her dead husband. In 1950, the bicentenary of Wesley's marriage to Molly Vazeille was fast approaching and, on 30 November, the *Sunderland Echo* carried an article exploring the dynamics between Elizabeth Hobson and John Wesley's admiration of her. The writer acknowledged Elizabeth's reputation, admitting that she was 'apparently a first-rate medium'.

John Wesley was in many respects an eccentric character, and not only because of his views on spirit communication. He was extremely superstitious, believing that thunderclaps were attacks of the Devil and that laughter was bad for the soul.

Still, we must not throw the baby out with the bath water, as they say. The eighteenth century was a far more superstitious time than our own in many ways, and Wesley's several eccentricities should not detract from his appraisal of Elizabeth's skills as a medium. She was a young woman who, it seems, had a number of special spiritual gifts that she bravely portrayed to an often-antagonistic public. Wesley, for all his faults, had the courage to recognise them and defend her.

I'll finish this story confident in the knowledge that when it's published they'll both be sitting reviewing it studiously in the afterlife. If either or both of them want to pop over from the other side and let me know what they think, they will be well and truly welcome.

Haunted Wardrobes

Many years ago, a resident of Rotherham Road in Sunderland bought a set of old wardrobes and placed them in her bedroom. Initially she was quite pleased with her purchase, but shortly after was stunned to see the ghost of an old woman standing by them. Almost as soon as it had appeared, the spectre vanished.

One evening, the lady of the house had been out with her sister-in-law and on their return to the house, they were greeted by the ghost in a most unseemly manner. At the top of the stairwell stood an ornamental vase filled with dried bulrushes. Just after they had walked through the front door, the bulrushes were removed from the vase by invisible hands and hurled down the stairs at the unsuspecting women.

The witnesses thought that a burglar was in the house, so they rushed up the stairs to confront what they believed was the thief. They could see no one, so they decided to make a systematic search of each room. The first room they entered was the one containing the wardrobes. To their utter astonishment, as they walked into the room the doors of the wardrobes flung open violently and the contents were hurled all over the room. Terrified, the women fled back downstairs. Once they had reached the relative safety of the hallway, the women looked back up the stairwell. There gazing down at them was the old woman.

The ghost appeared several times more and eventually the householder realised that the apparition was in some way connected to the wardrobes. She promptly sold them, and the old woman never appeared again.

Love and Fate

Just outside of Sunderland there is a large house that is now a residential establishment for the elderly, but at one time belonged to a wealthy Victorian industrialist.

Some years ago, during a torrential downpour of rain, three staff members were on night duty. Having completed their routine check of the premises they settled down with a cup of tea when, suddenly the lights in the staff room began to flicker. It was possible that the problem was due to the storm, of course, but one of the nurses decided to check things out just in case. The building had several storeys, each level lit by a pale blue night-light during the hours of darkness. The nurse made her way to the upper floor and proceeded to walk along a corridor. At one point, she happened to glance out of the window at the garden below and, just for a split second, thought that she saw something move. Then everything went still again, so she moved on. However, as she proceeded down the corridor she was suddenly confronted by an old lady wrapped in a grey shawl. Presuming that she was a resident who had been disturbed by the flickering light – or perhaps the foul weather – the nurse gently called to her not to be alarmed and to go back to bed.

Seemingly ignoring the nurse's request, the old lady drew nearer to the younger woman who was suddenly taken aback; as she looked at her face she realised that this old lady was not one of the residents. Without warning, she was overwhelmed with an icy cold feeling that swept over her entire body. Instinctively, she covered her face with her hands, at which

point the elderly woman stretched forth her own hand and touched the nurse's fingers. The old woman's hand was as cold as frost.

Sensing that something was not right, the nurse backed away into a nearby recess. Then, the old lady carried on her way down the corridor and, eventually, turned a corner which led her to the attic rooms. The nurse regained her composure and ran after the old woman, but when she turned the corner herself there was no one there, just a locked door that the woman could not have opened. The strange thing was that there was nowhere else the woman could have gone. She had, quite simply, disappeared into thin air.

Alarmed, the nurse summoned the other staff members and told them what had happened. They, too, were unable to supply an answer to the mystery. However, further enquiries revealed that other staff members had seen the same old lady moving about the building. The question, of course, was who was she? Seemingly, during the Victorian era, the daughter of the owner of the house had fallen in love with a man of whom her parents strongly disapproved. The twenty-seven-year old woman decided to elope with her sweetheart in the dead of night. Legend has it that the girl fatally injured herself as they made their escape by climbing over the back garden wall. Another version has her strict father, fearful of a scandal, packing her off to the Far East where he had extensive business interests, and in due course, she had died from a tropical disease.

Now her sad ghost supposedly haunts the old home – eternally seeking her true love from whose hands she was so cruelly taken. The problem with this idea is that the woman was said to be in her late twenties when she died, whereas the ghost who walks the corridor of that old mansion is obviously far, far, older. Whether they are connected or not, the place does seem to be haunted.

The 'Sunderland One'

Trains and train stations are intrinsically tied up with the haunting phenomenon, and the old Central Train Station in Sunderland is no exception. Mind you, I am not surprised as it has a bit of a gory history. In April 1888, Joseph Ankers, a painter from Newcastle, was decorating the station when he slipped and fell 40ft to his death. In July 1899, Stephen Hall of 44 Westbourne Avenue, Gateshead, was killed by a lift hoist near the north exit steps. The blow he received to his head was so severe that his skull was smashed into small pieces, while bits of his brain tissue apparently splattered over a wide area. In August 1913, a driver from Arnott Street in Hendon was hit by a steam engine as he took a short cut over the line. The impact was so severe that both of his legs were sliced off. Bleeding profusely, as one might imagine, he was rushed to the local infirmary where he died shortly thereafter.

Of all tragedies connected to the station, however, that of sixty-four-year-old George Buckley was probably the most gruesome. Buckley had been a successful actor, but his career was ruined when a First World War air raid on London shattered his eardrums. The resulting handicap was devastating and forced him into a downward spiral of poverty. Eventually, he was unable to pay his rent and, facing eviction from his lodgings at 16 Derwent Street, the poor chap decided that he had had enough.

In July 1923, the troubled thespian walked to the entrance of the station's tunnel and waited patiently. Then, as a train arrived, he lay down calmly and placed his head upon the line. The train driver suddenly saw what lay ahead of him, but was unable to stop. A wheel of the engine sliced through the neck and his severed head rolled to one side.

Buckley was not the only man to take his life in the station precincts. In September 1901, a forty-nine-year-old man from Stockton boarded a train in South Shields and took his seat in the first-class carriage. As the train pulled into Central Station in Sunderland, he pulled out a gun and placed the barrel in his mouth. Seconds later a shot rang out. A porter jumped onto the train and found the man with the gun at his side. The bullet was later found lodged in the fabric of the carriage behind – it had passed straight through his skull.

The spectres of all those mentioned, and more, have been said to haunt the

Sunderland Central Station; said to be host to a number of ghosts, including a dog known as 'the Sunderland One'. (Courtesy of Newcastle Libraries and Information Service)

station, but perhaps the most celebrated phantasm is that of a dog. 'Jack' was owned by a man from Hylton Castle and had a reputation for mischievous, impish behaviour. Starting in 1895, the canine repeatedly ran away from home and, for reasons not quite clear, invariably made his way to Central Station. Exasperated staff would conscientiously return him to his owner in the full and certain knowledge that he would be back again within days. In fact, the station became the dog's second home.

Once Jack realised that the staff were prepared to allow him to stay at their workplace, his confidence – and cheek – grew markedly. He began to hitch rides on steam trains until he had an unfortunate accident and broke a bone. The staff each chipped in the princely sum of 1*d* and hired a vet to take care of him. The broken bone was reset and a bandage was strapped around the joint, but as soon as the vet departed, Jack tore the dressing off. The vet replaced the bandage repeatedly, but to no avail. Within minutes, Jack removed the dressing again. Eventually the vet explained to the staff that the dog's refusal to keep the bandage in place was complicating matters and that he really had no option but to put the creature down.

With due reverence, Jack was transported to a stable in Green Street where the vet would put him down with poison. Jack, sensing that something wasn't quite right, broke free and escaped. The vet then hit upon the appalling idea of drowning the dog once he was recaptured. So a large barrel was filled with water by the entrance to the railway tunnel in readiness for the grim deed. Jack was brought to the place of his intended demise, but at that moment, a passing train distracted the vet and the staff and Jack made yet another successful bid for freedom. The Sunderland One, as he was known, was fast becoming a legend.

For some strange reason, the vet and rail staff seemed to think that by changing their intended mode of dispatching Jack to the afterlife they would increase their chances of success. The problem was not how they were going to kill him, but how to hang on to him long enough to do the deed. On the third attempt, the vet chose to hang Jack with a hemp rope, but yet again the fates were kind to Jack, who wriggled free and went on the run for another three days. Exasperated, both the vet and the station staff decided that a higher power seemed to want Jack very much alive, and, not wanting to upset the Almighty, they gave the dog a reprieve. At the time, they commented that such an intelligent dog – who knew exactly at what time each train drew into the station and would then bound along the platforms to meet it – thoroughly deserved to have his life spared. Unfortunately, it was whilst running to meet an incoming train that Jack met an untimely end. Whilst crossing the tracks, a second train was being shunted into a siding – a last-minute decision that cost Jack his life, for it hit him and cut him clean in two. The human ghosts at Central Station truly existed, but what about canine ones? Did Jack return to haunt the Central Station that he loved so dearly? He did indeed.

In 1891, a porter at the station saw Jack racing along the platform as fast as his legs could carry him, and another employee allegedly saw him standing next to the ticket office. He walked towards the dog and as he drew closer, it simply disappeared. Both employees had known Jack when he was alive and categorically stated that it was the legendary 'Sunderland One' they had seen. The story of Jack has largely faded from the public's memory now, but by writing up his story in this book, my hope is that it will be preserved for future generations; as I hope all of the tales told herein will be.

The Spooky Books of Southwick

Back in the 1970s, a general dealership near Southwick was subjected to some rather strange phenomena that, understandably, discomfited the owners greatly. It began when the till in the shop suddenly sprang open of its own accord and began ringing in payments for sales that had never taken place. Shortly after this, the sound of 'a ruler being snapped in half' was heard and a spoon was found bent and twisted.

After that, one of the owners refused to work in the store alone. The straw

Ghost Books – said to have been the reason for an outbreak of paranormal activity that broke out in a bookshop in Southwick in Sunderland back in the 1970s.

that broke the camel's back, so to speak, was when she opened up the shop one morning and found that all the fittings had been moved into one corner of the store, and a free-standing display of potato crisps had been turned around. When she found all of the greetings cards thrown from their shelf onto the floor the following morning, she had finally had enough.

So, what had precipitated this outbreak? Apparently, the chap who ran the shop had started selling books, some of which dealt with horoscopes and a number of 'occult' subjects. The paranormal phenomena apparently began when they started selling them, and stopped, just as abruptly, when they removed them from the shelves.

An artist's impression (nothing that is meant to bear resemblance to the original work) of the crying boy picture that was said to be cursed and caused mayhem and misery back in the 1980s. (Courtesy of Julie Olley)

The Crying Boy

Years ago, a veritable plague of paranormal activity swept the United Kingdom and Europe when prints of a number of pictures were alleged to be cursed. The paintings all featured haunting images of a crying boy. Those who hung the pictures in their home started to experience mysterious fires, and one newspaper even urged readers to send the pictures to them so that they could be incinerated on a bonfire.

The curse of the crying boy affected a number of families in the region, including one from Southwick. From the day they hung it up they seemingly had nothing but bad luck. They had

purchased the picture in 1982. Alan Tedder told Mike Hallowell that it seemed to be 'the eerie image of a disaster just waiting to be unleashed on all who came in contact with it'.

Previous owners of the picture claimed that they had experienced a number of unexplained fires and, although their property suffered from extensive damage, the print escaped harm. The Southwick couple who owned it in 1982 stated that a fire had broken out downstairs while they were sleeping. The bad luck seemed to worsen, as their daughter's search for a house of her own was unsuccessful, and the relationship between the daughter and her boyfriend had hit the rocks. Then, the father, who had seemingly been in the best of health, suffered a serious heart attack.

Eventually the print of the crying boy was consigned to the dustbin, and normality returned.

A Haunted Factory

Some years ago, an elderly chap who lived in London returned to Sunderland, the place of his birth. He had not been home since the 1930s and decided to take a stroll down memory lane by revisiting some of the old places he had known as a teenager.

One such place was an old factory unit in the city centre, where he had worked as a young lad, and as he stood looking at its fading paintwork and deteriorating roof he recalled that it was at one time reputed to be haunted. His brother had also worked there and both of them had been afraid to go to the top floor of the building, as it was allegedly inhabited by the spectre of a woman.

During the Second World War, a woman happened to be passing the factory during the blackout and was surprised to see a young couple emerge from one of the doorways, arms linked. What shocked her, though, was that they subsequently walked through the wall behind them and promptly disappeared.

The Haunted Undertakers

A firm of undertakers in Sunderland once operated from a former assembly hall in the town centre. Ever since they had moved into the premises, staff had heard repeated rumours that they were haunted. However, one young employee seemed to sense the presence of the ghost more than most. He always felt particularly uncomfortable on the second floor, which, it later transpired, was haunted by a female ghost of unknown provenance.

The Haunted Vault of Low Street

The Vault was a rather grim property that stood a mere 4 yards to the east of the Customs House. In the late eighteenth and early nineteenth centuries, it was also nicknamed 'The Cell', because it used to house various ne'er-do-wells waiting for their appearance before the courts.

The roof of the Vault was 3ft below the surface of the street, and it was, therefore, technically subterranean. There was no shortage of tales that told of the building being haunted by the spectres of those vagabonds who had died there – and there had been quite a few. There was also a rumour that smugglers used to store contraband there and had invented the ghost stories to dissuade the Customs & Excise men. A technique that had been used with considerable success at an old pub in South Shields called The Hop Pole.

The Heavy Breathing Ghost

In November 1967, several walkers happened to pass by a Catholic school late one night in Sunderland when, as they neared the gatehouse, they heard the eerie sound of someone sighing or perhaps breathing heavily. Not long afterwards, a man walking his Alsatian dog alleged that the beast became so disconcerted at the same spot that it refused to go any further. The only way its owner could persuade the dog to move forwards was by taking him to the other side of the road. On the return journey, the man and his dog passed right next to the gate, but this time his canine companion behaved perfectly normally.

A third witness was a woman who claimed that she too heard the sighs and heavy breaths as she passed, and stated that they seemed to be emanating from the gatekeeper's cottage. (Before you start making your own jokes up and reaching highly unwarranted conclusions, please remember that it was November and the windows would almost certainly have been closed.)

At 8 p.m. that same day, several youths passed by and all of them heard the same eerie noises. Like the woman who had heard them earlier, they claimed they were coming from the gatekeeper's cottage.

Meg Shipley's Spectre

There is quite a prestigious club in Sunderland that was reputedly haunted. In November 1986, members admitted that some strange things were going on; lights in the basement were switching on and off, and on one occasion the assistant secretary went to put his key in the lock of a door, and as he did so it rattled so violently it was a wonder it did not fly off its hinges. No one, of course, was on the other side.

Other spooky things happened, including an occasion when a cleaner put disinfectant cubes in a urinal bowl – as soon as her back was turned, they were removed and placed in the next bowl along. If there were any doubts about whether this was paranormal activity, they were dismissed when the toilet in one of the cubicles started to flush by itself. The episode with the disinfectant cubes is almost identical to others experienced by staff at the Marsden Grotto Inn a few miles down the road, where the cubes were not transferred from one urinal to another, but actually arranged in delightful geometric patterns on the tiled floor.

The concert room was also subjected to strange happenings. Staff heard the sound of humming and whistling even when the room was empty, and the drum kit on the stage shook violently. Disembodied footsteps were also noted on numerous occasions, particularly on the stairs, and a secretary reported disconcerting and unexplained temperature drops in the same room.

Descriptions of the ghost were not exactly detailed, but they were reasonably consistent. It was invariably described as female and clothed in black, although sometimes invisible from the waist down. One of the committee members happened to be passing the service lift in the concert room and was somewhat taken aback when what he described as 'a hazy apparition' rushed past him. For some reason, the overwhelming consensus was that the ghost was that of a woman called Meg Shipley, who had frequented the premises in the early twentieth century. One elderly club member said that her grandmother had actually known Meg and testified that she always sat in a certain corner of the club, dressed in black.

Meg Shipley was known as a 'fishwife', due to her father's profession as a fisherman, and lived at 27 Norfolk Street. When Meg married, she became Margaret Lownes (or Lowndes, or Lownds, depending on which historical document takes your fancy). Born in 1877, she soon took to the fishing business with gusto and purchased large consignments of fish that she would then sell on to forty other fishwives. She also earned the princely sum of 1*d* an hour by curing kippers, and supplemented her income even further by selling shellfish on the corner of Bridge Street and West Wear Street in the year 1908. Meg appears to have been a tough old boot and went about her business in the most inclement weather.

Even in the 1990s, workers at the club reported seeing the apparition of a woman in a cloak ascending the stairs, although whether she has been seen since then I do not know.

An artist's impression of the ghost lady in black that was seen fading from the waist down in Sunderland in 1986. (Courtesy of Julie Olley)

The Wet Lady of Roker Park

In October 1942, two Sunderland men reported seeing the 'floating figure' of a woman at Roker Park. She seemed to be calm, contented and at peace. In fact, the only thing odd about her appearance (apart from the fact that she was partly transparent, of course) was that she was dripping with water, as if she had just crawled out of the nearby pond. The two men took to their heels and ran.

In July 1963, Margaret Fanakam and her friend Stajoni Bliver, from

The lake in Roker Park in Sunderland where a number of witnesses claimed to see a 'soaking wet and floating ghostly figure' wearing a night dress, back in 1942 and in 1963 respectively.

Welcome to **ROKER PARK**

Denmark, visited Sunderland for a holiday, and one Saturday morning they visited Roker Park. There they had a most disturbing experience. Both women saw the 'spirit' of a female ghost in a long nightdress covered by a thick coat and said that she appeared to be 'wet through'.

Just who was the Wet Lady of Roker Park, then? It is possible that the sightings could be linked to the death of a sixty-year-old teacher from Redby School who was, tragically, found floating in the lake at Roker Park. She had left her home in Sea View Gardens several nights previously, and concerns had been expressed for her welfare. When her body was pulled from the water she was wearing only her nightdress and a fur coat – remarkably similar to the description given of the Wet Lady by Margaret and Stajoni.

It seems that the woman pulled from the lake had committed suicide and had entered the park at night when it was closed.

Another area of Roker Park said to be haunted was that known as 'The Ravine', where, in October 1950, two schoolboys found the skeleton of a small (5ft) adult male that had been buried there for around 200 years. There were no signs of injury to the skeleton, and the cause of death could not be determined.

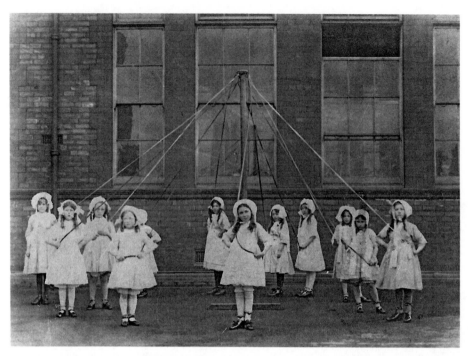

Girls of Redby School playing around the Maypole. (Courtesy of Newcastle Libraries and Information Service)

The Ravine in Roker Park where another ghost is reputed to walk although details of this ghost are scant.

A Ghostly Warning

Castletown Colliery met its demise many moons ago, but during its life it developed an unenviable reputation for being haunted. One night, a group of miners were about to begin their shift and were heading for the coalface with a deputy overman. As they passed a shaft, several of the pitmen noticed what they thought was a faint flicker of light deep inside. The deputy, somewhat puzzled, accompanied the men to the coalface and then returned to the tunnel to investigate.

The tunnel in question had not been worked for many years and he stumbled over the detritus that had accumulated on the ground, studiously trying to figure out where the light had emanated from. Suddenly, a faint but distinct smell entered his nostrils – toxic fumes. According to Alan Tedder: 'Investigation revealed that one of the safety doors which should have been sealed was open and annoyed at this lapse, he stepped through it, closed it behind him then went deeper into the passage.'

At that point, his safety lamp began to splutter. The deputy, sensing that an explosion may occur, noticed that a door that should have been shut was in fact wide open, he closed it firmly and, according to Tedder, 'proceeded to dampen the potential danger to the miners at work'. Later, he came to believe that a miner of old had returned in ghostly form to alert his present-day workmates to the danger in the tunnel. Had the ghost somehow generated that faint sparkle of light to warn the living of the danger? We may never know.

The Washington Witch

During the reign of James I, witch-hunting was a popular pastime that led to many innocent people being executed in the most barbaric fashion. One such victim was Jane Atkinson, also known as the Washington Witch. Atkinson was accused of witchcraft and suffered the terrible agony of the 'water test', otherwise known as 'ducking'; she was immersed in water in the belief that if she drowned she must have been innocent, and if she survived it was a sure sign of guilt, so she would then be executed anyway. Those who testified against the accused were often paid a pretty penny, thus demolishing any pretence of impartiality during these obscene trials.

It is thought by some that Atkinson survived the water test, which was carried out in Washington Village green, where the war memorial now stands, and was thus duly executed in 1696, although some accounts of this tale inform us that she actually drowned in the local pond during the 'test'. Whatever occurred, her body was later buried under the shade of an oak tree, where her ghost has been seen on numerous occasions.

Washington Green in Washington; the war memorial stands on the site of the old village pond where it is said that a 'ducking' took place to determine whether or not a local woman was a witch.

Washington Art Centre

The art centre in Fatfield, Washington, is a strange old place. Once the site of an ancient farm, the art centre is now a modern establishment offering its visitors a gallery, artists' studios, a recording studio, a theatre, function rooms, tearooms, bar and much more.

Many of the ancient farm buildings are incorporated into the modern centre giving it a well-worn and old-world look. Indeed, this is just one of the many reasons why the local folk think the establishment is haunted.

The most well-known tale of ghosts at the art centre goes back to 1994, and concerns a novel, coin-operated device that takes pictures with a fitted Polaroid camera. One morning, the staff turned up at the centre for work to discover that a photograph had been taken through the night and had been left dispensed from the machine. More chillingly, when they looked at the photograph they were surprised to see a woman with long hair looking directly into the camera. It must be stressed that, when the staff locked up the night before no one was in the building and when they opened the following morning everything was in its place. The alarms had not tripped, and CCTV cameras filmed no intruders, yet it seemed a misty looking woman activated the coin-operated device and had her picture taken.

Other things have been experienced at the art centre too. It is said that a woman committed suicide by hanging herself from the wooden beams and is believed to haunt the theatre area of the complex. A week before my visit in May 2004, staff had seen dark figures making their way up and down the main staircase, and glasses had been thrown from the counter when there was nobody near them. This information was reported to me after my visit with the bar staff and cleaners, who had actually heard the glasses smash in the empty room.

I will now recite the harrowing account of what happened to me during an all-night investigation at the centre. I was working with two quite well-known ghost hunters at that time, Glen Clough and Danny Jones. We were also working with Martin, Charlotte and the manager, Pauline, who were members of staff and guests

of the investigation. We had split up into groups to investigate the building.

When we went into the theatre area, Glen Clough suggested we should try an experiment to see if we could make contact with the alleged spirits. We tried a table tipping experiment. I thought it would be a good chance to have a go at spirit communication, so I jumped at the chance. I was then asked if I could lead the experiment while he observed. I said that was fine, so we found a table that was ideal for the job. It was small, light, and thus easy for the spirits to tip and move (for that is the general idea). We got comfortable and sat around the table. Myself, Martin and Charlotte rested our hands on the table and joined fingers, keeping

The Washington Art Centre in Fatfield, Washington.

Another view of the Washington Art Centre in Fatfield. The author had one of the strangest nights here back in May 2004.

our thumbs up and away from the table itself. The circle (similar to a séance) is said to give the alleged spirits the positive and collective energy required to move or tip the table. Glen began the proceedings by getting us to concentrate on our breathing and getting us relaxed by asking us to close our eyes and concentrate on the 'in and out breaths'. After a while, he asked me to call to the alleged spirits, to see if they could make their presences known.

No sooner had I said, 'If there are any spirits in the room with us tonight', I suddenly became extremely dizzy and disorientated, and it was not nice at all. I was not sure what was actually going on. It came on very quickly to say the least, but I persevered for a few more minutes. Then I felt a tremendous pain in my neck, which ran down the length of my back. I was in total agony and my still head was still spinning. Then, if that was not bad enough, my vision became distorted and blurred. I felt very uneasy and quite frightened, as you can imagine, so at that point I asked if I could take a break. I thought something was going wrong with me on a physical level, like a seizure or something of that nature, but that was not the case ... thankfully.

Ten minutes or so later, after I had left the room at the request of the other investigators, I felt better. My dizziness had ceased and my vision had returned to normal. I explained to the group that I was not psychic (at least not in the Doris Stokes or Tony Stockwell sense) and I had never felt anything like that before on an investigation (or at any time for that matter). I told the others that if there was a spirit, it was certainly letting me know 'it' was there. I got the impression that whoever the spirit was, they had suffered the pain that I had just felt. I felt as though I was being hanged! It was then that Pauline told us that other visiting mediums had picked up and sensed those exact feelings. I reiterated the fact that I was not a medium and if what I had experienced was indeed psychic, 'then they could keep it!' Pauline then told us that a woman was thought to have hanged herself in the courtyard bar and that this area had often been haunted by her.

If you think about this for a minute, the symptoms I felt that night are very similar to those who slowly hang. As the oxygen supply to the brain depletes you begin to feel disorientated. This would be followed by loss of vision and dizziness. Neck pain and other pains down the spine would soon follow due to the rope being held tight around the neck and throat. This is an awful way to pass over and at times it can take up to fifteen minutes to die. Was I picking up on this woman's final moments of her physical life as she was dying? I think I was, and this was backed up by the fact that I said, 'I felt as though I was being hanged', even before I knew about the actual suicide by hanging.

This is probably one of the most frightening physical experiences I have had during my years of investigating haunted properties. I am not a spirit medium, nor do I claim to have psychic powers that I can conjure up at will. I am a normal, everyday person that experienced something that was certainly 'not normal', and I believe wholeheartedly that I sensed the spirit of that dying woman. Furthermore, I really believe that I felt the pain and suffering that she would have felt during the last moments of her life. I am convinced that the theatre in the arts centre really could have provided me with some form of proof of the afterlife that night.

Washington Old Hall

Washington Old Hall is located in Washington Village and dates back to Saxon times. It was once owned by the relatives of George Washington. Formerly owned by the Bishop of Durham, the estate at Washington was exchanged during the twelfth century and when it came into the possession of the first 'William of Washington'. The Hall was built on to the original building many years after it was constructed, and by the end of the nineteenth century it was used as living quarters for around thirty or so people; they lived in dreadful, overcrowded conditions. Today, it is open to the public and is owned by the National Trust.

This particular building was always said to have only the one ghost – a sad-looking woman known as the 'Grey Lady'. She is said to pace the upper floors of the hall and has been seen

Washington Old Hall in Washington Village; said to be haunted by a 'Grey Lady' that is thought to date back hundreds of years.

countless times by the hall staff with her head bent over, weeping.

The Old Hall is yet another incredible location that I have had the privilege of spending a whole night in and with some very interesting results. Most of the night's activities were slow and boring as you would expect, and it was not until the early hours of the next morning things began to pick up. A number of group séances were held in a panelled room, with some very odd paranormal phenomena being documented. An old colleague of mine was present on the night and witnessed some of the ghostly goings on. He says:

Can I just say that we had two séances and we got responses to every question with loud bangs in that corner of the room (referring to the corner where the spinning wheel is). The trigger objects moved twice and there was a shadow moving across the wall and it was seen by all of us. I got touched, and two other investigators also got touched, when we tried it again she [the spirit] came back again and we could all hear her moving around the room and we know everyone was accounted for and in their place. We could hear something in and around the room by footsteps upon the creaking floorboards. The vase in the middle of the table in which we had the circle actually moved and we all heard it slide across the table. I am a very sceptical investigator, but something was definitely happening in there.

I was also informed by my colleague that he and another investigator heard noises that would indicate movement coming from within the empty pan-elled room, whilst they were in the kitchen area of the hall. They had both heard loud knocks, mysterious bumps and the unmistakable sound of shuf-fling feet. A disembodied sigh or breath emanated from within the empty room too, which rattled them both some-what. This incident occurred on a break between two séances that were held in this particular room.

Of course, they then made the deci-sion to look into the room and try to work out exactly what was going on in there. When they both rushed into the panelled room, they both saw something drift across the chamber and then disap-pear through the oak-panelled walls.

My old colleague described the apparition to me as, 'A four to five foot tall shimmering grey mist with little sparkles in it'. Both investigators were clearly surprised by this 'grey mist sighting' and both came across as very excited. In all honesty, they were ecstatic about the whole experience.

To me, of course, this adds a little credibility to the haunting of Washington Old Hall. I know this investigator very well indeed and trust him completely. If he and his co-inves-tigator claimed they saw 'something' then I believe them. Indeed, while I was in that room later on, taking part in another experiment, I too heard the blatant knocks and bumps, footsteps and shuffling of something other-worldly making its presence known, and that is my testimony. A number of people on the night heard a vase sliding along the table when no one was close to it, this seems to indicate an energy, or a presence of some sort, being at work in there.

This raises a few questions in rela-tion to the ghost of the hall. Earlier on, I stated that this building only had one ghost, but the 'Grey Lady' has always been known to appear on the upper level of the building and was always thought to be a playback ghost, or a stone tape ghost. This is a common theory that suggests the building where the ghost is seen acts as a video recorder and somehow plays back a moment of history, such as somebody's movements or actions; as in this case, a lady walking along a corridor. These sightings remain the same time and again; they do not talk, interact with you, nor do they change their stature or their appearance.

If the ghost of the 'Grey Lady' of Washington Old Hall is a 'psychic recording' and is confined to the upper levels of the building, then what, or who, was the apparition that my col-leagues had seen? Could it have been another ghost of the hall taking the ghost count to two? It could well be, however, the Grey Lady making her presence known downstairs in the hall, eliminating the notion that she is a stone tape ghost or a psychic record-ing. I think either way we have learned something new about the ghost, or ghosts, of Washington Old Hall.

Another view of Washington Old Hall.

The panelled room at Washington Old Hall.

The Ghostly Soldier of Ryhope Green

According to legend, the ghostly soldier of Ryhope Green made his first appearance on All Hallows' Eve in 1926. Witnesses claimed that they had first spotted him at the eastern aspect of the green and described him as a small, stocky figure wearing a black skullcap. In one hand he carried a lit candle and in the other a pick. Even though a strong breeze was blowing, observers noticed that the candle flame never flickered or went out. Within a minute or two, the strange figure walked towards the War Memorial on the green and set the candle down. Then, using the pick, he started to dig a hole. This went on for half an hour and during all that time the witnesses, although some distance away, looked on in morbid fascination. Once the hole was dug, the apparition jumped into it and promptly disappeared. All that was left behind when the observers eventually approached the hole was the waxy smell of the burning candle.

As one may well imagine, word of the incident spread throughout Ryhope like wildfire. A huge crowd gathered within the hour, but the spectre did not make a second appearance. By 2 a.m. the curiosity seekers started to disperse, along with a number of young scallywags who had taken to dancing about with picks and shovels in a crude imitation of the ghost. As things transpired, they should have hung around for a bit longer.

Less than an hour and a quarter after they returned to their dwellings, a lone reveller was making his way past the green when he saw the ghost in all its spectral glory. The man panicked and ran all the way home along a nearby railway track. Someone had witnessed the incident, and within minutes the crowds had started to return.

A rather robust individual from Sunderland, who fancied himself as a pugilist, stood in the middle of the green and boldly announced that he was there to 'challenge the ghost to a spot of fisticuffs'. The apparition was not listening, or maybe it did not fancy its chances with the tough guy from Sunderland, for it resolutely failed to show up.

An elderly lady from Ryhope, who had lived there all her life and was extremely knowledgeable regarding local folklore, pointed out that the haunting of Ryhope Green was not a new phenomenon. In fact, ghosts had been appearing on and off there for over three centuries. For some reason, the haunting only became active every twenty-five years. The woman had seen the ghost twice and on both occasions it had been leaving a property at the east end of the green.

Just who was the ghost, then? Nearby Ryhope Hall had once been a staging halt known as The Boars Head and was reputed to be a hangout for local highwaymen. Some even claim that the infamous Dick Turpin had once lodged there, but as Turpin is alleged to have lodged at just about

Ryhope Green, where the ghost of a soldier carrying a candle in one hand and a pick in the other is reported to have been seen in 1926.

any old pub in the United Kingdom it may not be wise to put too much stock in the tale. Another theory is that a hoax had been put about by a cheeky chancer called Lindon Laing, whose parents were caretakers at the local secondary school.

Laing, a journalist of some repute, penned an article in which he claimed that the ghost of a 'White Lady' some-times appeared on the green. She was, he said, a most pitiful sight, clutching her newborn child to her breast and weeping plaintively over some dark tragedy in her life. Those who wished to see her had best visit the location of the horse trough on the green, he intimated, for that was where she most often showed herself. Of course, there was no 'White Lady', although that did not stop dozens of locals coming forth

in all seriousness and claiming they had seen her. Alas, the genie could not be put back in the bottle and the 'White Lady of Ryhope Green' is still seen from time to time.

Did Laing also create the story of the ghost that appeared on Halloween in 1926? Who knows, I suspect not though as there were numerous witnesses who saw the spectre simul-taneously.

The most common belief regarding the Ryhope Green ghost, however, has nothing to do with Lindon Laing. It is said that the soldier from Ryhope who fought and died in the First World War had his name accidentally omit-ted from the list on the War Memorial. His ghost had threatened to haunt the green for all eternity – or at least, until justice was done and his name was honoured along with all the others. Some researchers have suggested that the apparition seen in 1926 was not wearing a 'skullcap' at all, but actually a tin helmet. As for the candle, could it not have been a torch?

The ghost of much earlier provenance, seen on two occasions walking from the property at the other end of the green, is not thought to be connected to the soldier. By 1932, the site of Ryhope Hall had been assumed by a working men's club called Robson's Place. Prior to this, however, when the hall was still a private residence, a squire had committed suicide after the termination of an intense relationship with his girlfriend. It is the ghost of the squire, allegedly, which is seen at this location every twenty-five years.

The North East (Sunderland) Aircraft Museum

The North East Aircraft Museum in Sunderland is one of the venues in the region that I had always wanted to investigate since I began my ghost research many years ago. The land in which the North East Aircraft Museum is situated is said to be next to the site of an ancient Roman burial ground. The museum itself was once an airfield during the First World War and then a fighter station, known as RAF Usworth, during Second World War. Two squadrons were based at Usworth – 607 Squadron and 55 Operational Training Unit (O.T.U.). The aircraft museum, which is probably one of the largest in the country, houses over thirty magnificent types of aircraft that are in various stages of restoration. Along with these aircraft, the museum houses a number of displays that reflect aviation history across the north east region and beyond.

For those that have read my other books, *Ghost Hunter* (2006) and *Paranormal North East* (2009), you will be aware that I once investigated an alleged haunted B2 Canberra Bomber cockpit after the owner (an aviation enthusiast named Karl Edmondson) contacted a friend of mine, who in turn handed the case over to me. Ever since I took that investigation on and got to grips with the actual aeroplane, I became fascinated with aviation itself and with the thought of certain ghosts, spirits or energies, being attached to these machines.

It is funny really, the aircraft museum has been on this site, and so close to home, yet I had never visited the place. Upon my arrival at 11.30 p.m. on 31 January 2009, I made a conscious effort to talk to the site manager, Keith Davison, to find out about the ghosts that are said to reside there. Before finding Keith, or anyone one else for that matter, I meandered into the main hangar where the gift shop is, in an effort to find everyone, and ended up having a strange and unnerving experience of my own.

I walked in to find the gift shop and main entrance area completely empty so decided to venture through the doors into the display area. No one was there, so I continued on to the main hangar area where there were dozens of aircraft on display. It was very dark and I thought the first vigils of the night must have commenced. Not wanting to disturb these vigils, but in the same respect wanting to let the team know that my colleague and I had arrived, I called out to see if anyone was in the hangar, and got no answer. I then called out again. Still there was no reply. I was about to turn and walk back out when I suddenly heard the shuffling of feet and the sound of footfalls coming from the back of the hangar, behind the planes.

I shouted out once more, but yet again I had no response and the sound of the footsteps continued. I walked further into the hangar, calling out for my colleagues at the same time, until I noticed that the footsteps I had been hearing had ceased. I then realised I was in this hangar on my own with no other acquaintance of mine being present. Feeling a little unnerved and after making sure no one was in there,

The North East Aircraft Museum, Wearside.

I left and eventually found everyone else awaiting our arrival in the base room that stood in another smaller building near the car park. I realised I had heard what I now presume to be ghostly footfalls.

After eventually making my way to the correct office, I decided to talk to the manager in an effort to glean some history and some ghost stories for my research notes. After getting permission to feature the museum in this book, I asked Keith about the ghosts. In a recorded interview he went on to tell me:

With two squadrons once being based here and with one of them being the 55 O.T.U. Squadron group, there was of course lots of training accidents. On one day it is said that six RAF men died in a horrific accident and in my opinion you get a lot of activity here at Usworth. Those men are said to still walk the area haunting the place; they were thought to have been seen during the actual war not long after they died. We also get a lot of WAF's coming back too (Women of the Royal Air Force) with the sound of their singing and piano playing as they rejoice with camaraderie. I have actually heard them singing myself. We have another ghost named Flight Sergeant Shaw who haunts the main hangar after we had dug up his engine; we had actually brought his spirit here with it. We also have the ghost of a chap called Sergeant Green, and he too arrived with wreckage from one of our aircraft

Old aircraft stand disused and on display outside the haunted hangars of the North East Aircraft Museum.

on display here. There is also the ghost of a Canadian airman in the other hangar across the way and he is seen on a regular basis. In hangar two it is said that if you rest your hands upon the aircraft that is housed in there, the phantom owner of the plane rocks the plane out of disapproval. So yes, we do have a lot of ghosts that reside here at the museum; in fact, I often see them when I least expect it and it is usually when I am not looking for them.

After chatting with Keith, I realised that if all these ghost stories were true accounts, the site could indeed be very haunted. Keith is a reliable source of information and with his, and countless other testimonies, we must reasonably assume the place is indeed haunted. I also particularly like the idea of spirit people coming in to the museum that

are allegedly attached to their particular plane wreckage – a very interesting concept indeed, albeit not a new one, as I have heard other accounts of this occurring in many other instances.

In regards to our investigation there, there is only one account that I would like to include here. It occurred as we ventured into the hangar to begin a vigil. I always take notes via my dictation device nowadays, as once upon a time I would spend the entire night with my head down scribbling notes about what everyone else was reporting, hearing or seeing and very rarely did I get 'vigil time' to myself. I figured if I used a dictation device (EVP machine), I could speak my notes into the machine, record what is generally going on and get my much needed 'observation time'. Anyway, as I started to call out I began to take dictation notes for my write-ups. The vigil lasted one hour and it proved rather interesting to say the least. As I was listening back to this section of the tape in my office at home, a day or so after the investigation, I was amazed to hear an anomalous voice speaking over (or in between) mine. You can hear me announcing clearly on the tape that it was 'vigil two' and I had joined the others; after I call out to a guest investigator, you can hear a whispering voice on the recording simply saying 'Argies'. 'Argies' is a term for Argentineans, like 'Brits' is used for British people, and so the thought crossed my mind that one of the many planes housed in this hangar may have served in Argentina during the Falklands conflict.

You can imagine how surprised I was to find out after the investigation and during the compilation of this section, that one plane in particular, the FMA Pucara (A-522) that sits in this hangar, was one of twelve Pucaras that were once stationed in Port Stanley during the Falklands conflict around May 1982. They were there to replace the other aircraft that had been lost in the conflict and it was part of the Argentine Air Force's Grupo 3 de Ataque. They were kept there until the end of the war, whereupon it was shipped to the UK and eventually found its way to the North East Aircraft Museum in the summer of 1994. Was the anomalous voice saying 'Argies' and the connection to the Falklands conflict a coincidence or paranormal phenomena? You decide. Oh, and for the record, I was standing next to this very aircraft when I made the recording!

So, is the site haunted? I dare say it probably is, but a lot more investigating on a personal level would be required before coming to any definite conclusions, although I can safely suggest that something rather odd does indeed occur here at the north east's finest (and only) aircraft museum.

BIBLIOGRAPHY AND SOURCES

Books

Hallum, Jack, *Ghosts of the North* (David & Charles, 1976)

Hapgood, Sarah, *500 British Ghosts and Hauntings* (Foulsham, 1993)

Harries, John, *The Ghost Hunters Road Book* (Letts, 1968)

Hippisley Coxe, Antony A., *Haunted Britain* (Pan, 1973)

Matthews, Rupert, *Haunted Sunderland* (Stroud: The History Press, 2008)

Poole, Keith B., *Haunted Heritage* (Guild Publishing, 1988)

Puttick, Betty, *Supernatural England* (Countryside Books, 2002)

Price, Harry, *Poltergeist over England* (Country Life Ltd, 1945)

Ritson, Darren W., *Haunted Newcastle* (Stroud: The History Press, 2009)

—, *Ghost Hunter, True Life Encounters from the North East* (Grosvenor House Publishing, 2006)

—, *In Search of Ghosts, Real Hauntings from Around Britain* (Stroud: Amberley, 2008)

—, *Supernatural North* (Stroud: Amberley, 2009)

—, *Ghosts at Christmas* (Stroud: The History Press, 2010)

Robson, Alan, *Grisly Trails and Ghostly Tales* (Virgin Books, 1992)

Underwood, Peter, *This Haunted Isle* (Harrap, 1984)

—, *A Gazetteer or British Ghosts* (Souvenir Press, 1971)

—, *A-Z of British Ghosts* (Souvenir Press, 1971)

Websites

www.oldsunderland.co.uk
www.wearsideonline.com
www.herrington-heritage.org.uk
www.lostheritage.org.uk

If you enjoyed this book, you may also be interested in …

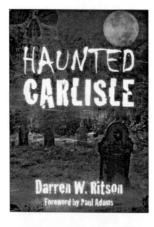

Haunted Carlisle

DARREN W. RITSON

This new book contains a chilling collection of eyewitness accounts and terrifying tales from in and around Carlisle which is sure to appeal to everyone interested in the supernatural history of the city.

Illustrated with over 60 pictures, these spooky stories include the headless spectre of Carlisle railway station, the phantom boy of Corby Castle, and the ghostly highwayman of Barrock Park, among many others. *Haunted Carlisle* is guaranteed to make your blood run cold.

978 0 7524 6087 1

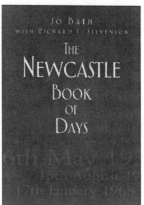

The Newcastle Book of Days

JO BATH WITH RICHARD F. STEVENSON

Taking you through the year day by day, *The Newcastle Book of Days* contains quirky, eccentric, amusing and important events and facts from different periods in the history of the city.

Ideal for dipping into, this addictive little book will keep you entertained and informed. Featuring hundreds of snippets of information gleaned from the vaults of Newcastle's archives and covering the social, criminal, political, religious, industrial, military and sporting history of the region, it will delight residents and visitors alike.

978 0 7524 6866 2

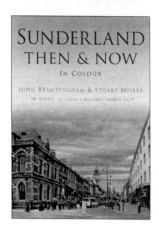

Sunderland Then & Now

JOHN BRANTINGHAM & STUART MILLER

The vibrant and cosmopolitan city of Sunderland has a rich heritage which is uniquely reflected in this fascinating new compilation. Contrasting a selection of 45 archive images alongside 45 full-colour modern photographs, this unique book captures how the city used to be and how it looks today. Accompanied by informative captions, each page captures life in the area as it once was - and is now. Featuring streets, buildings, shops, businesses and the people of Sunderland, all aspects of life in the city are covered, providing a fascinating insight into the changing face of the city. *Sunderland Then & Now* is a must for tourists, residents and local historians alike.

978 0 7524 6164 9

Visit our website and discover thousands of other History Press books.

www.thehistorypress.co.uk

Lightning Source UK Ltd.
Milton Keynes UK
UKOW030606060713

213336UK00001B/5/P